THIS EVANGELICAL LUTHERAN CHURCH OF OURS

To Inger

One of ours

Kenn Ward

Kenn Ward

Wood Lake Books

Editing: Jim Taylor, Michael Schwartzentruber
Design and layout: Michael Schwartzentruber
Cover design: Lois Huey-Heck

Photos: courtesy of *Canada Lutheran*

Canadian Cataloguing in Publication data

Ward, Kenn, 1946–

This Evangelical Lutheran Church of Ours

ISBN 0–929032–91–8

1. Evangelical Lutheran Church in Canada. I. Title.
BX8063.C2W37 1994   284.1'71   C94–910058–7

Published by
Wood Lake Books Inc.
P. O. Box 700, Winfield, BC
Canada V0H 2C0

Printed in Canada by
Hignell Printing Ltd.
Winnipeg, MB, R3G 2B4

Table of Contents

Foreword

This book is meant to be a conversation, one that you can pick up now and then, here and there. It is meant to be an introduction to the Lutheran church with all its history and practice. I think it is a good conversation and maybe can be a good conversation piece.

At the heart of Lutheran theology is a phrase by which we describe the human dilemma. We say that the redeemed are at the same time "saint and sinner." Kenn Ward is successful in getting at this to a degree— at least as successful as most of us when we try to speak on the subject. But there is a sense in which the idea is so radical and so concrete that it defies words.

This book also lifts up something of the differences that exist in Lutheranism itself. Kenn rightly underlines the fact that our theology has a healthy respect for unity in diversity and the ecumenical nature of the church. "We don't resolve things as clearly as some would like," he suggests. While that may not sit well with some who want their view to prevail, it is not unLutheran to live with the tension of opposing views in the body of Christ.

Luther was very open to discussing the authority of scripture, even to the point of suggesting that some books of the Bible were not as important as others. Many Lutherans, as Kenn suggests, can live with this open spirit about the Bible while others cannot.

The Lutheran Church that Kenn and I are part of calls itself "Evangelical." As he suggests, that has to do with "those who share good (or God's) news." Is this church sharing the good news? That's a question confronting members of our church. I invite you to enter into the conversation.

Telmor Sartison, Bishop of the
Evangelical Lutheran Church in Canada

Preface

This book began life as a clone of Ralph Milton's book, *This United Church of Ours*. But it soon took on a life of its own.

At first, I copied most of Ralph's topics and titles because there are many places where our two denominations are very similar. However, there are also ways in which we are each quite unique. I hope that at least a few people will take the time to read both books side by side and to ponder the comparisons and contrasts that they discover.

As I began, I had no idea how many people this project would involve, and I never fully understood why authors thank so many people at the beginning of their books. Now I know. While I want to acknowledge each person's contribution, please direct any criticism you may have at me and not at them.

There was Charlie Raine who generously provided a computer for my work. Tom Lurvey read the first draft of every chapter and offered many suggestions that helped to shape the direction I should take. My wife Diane, daughter Teri-Lyn, and son Jef provided a lot of support, encouragement and understanding, even if I didn't say as much about the perils of being pastor's kids as my kids would have liked. Even Caramel our cat got into the act every now and then.

Iris Siemens and John Tataryn provided valuable observations for "Learning to speak Lutheran." *Canada Lutheran* staff, Darrell Dyck, Liz Olson, Irene Pomes and Maureen Stokell, put up with me as I tried to do my regular job while writing this book on the side.

A number of friends, colleagues, and acquaintances provided insight, suggestions and necessary corrections for various sections and chapters. While I listened carefully to what each had to say, I didn't always heed their advice. That said, thank you: Jim Chell, ELCIC Division for Canadian Mission; Larry Denef, ELCIC Division for Theological Education; Diane Doth, Evangelical Lutheran Women; Leon Gilbertson, Secretary, ELCIC; Richard Husfloen, ELCIC Office for Resource Development; Ken Kuhn, ELCIC Division for Church and Society; Ed Lehman, President, Lutheran Church—Canada; Peter Mathiasen, ELCIC Division for World Mission; Cliff Monk, former Lutheran Council in Canada staff member; Joan Nolting, ELCIC Department of Finance and Administration; Eleanor Sander, ELCIC Division for Parish Life; Norman Threinen, professor, Concordia Lutheran Seminary, Edmonton; Larry Weckwerth, music director, Messiah, Winnipeg; and Fran Wershler, editor, *The Canadian Lutheran*.

Then there were a whole crew of special people who read a draft of the entire book and made many helpful suggestions which resulted in several modifications as I wrote the final draft: Phil Brose, Merv Campone, Jim and Maxine Hobden, Marge Knebel, Dan Klymchuk, Ilse Krentz, Richard Nostbakken, Vicki Schenk, Donald Sjoberg, Marquise Sopher, Sharon Villetard, and Pauline Weldon.

Getting started

Let me tell you a bit about the way I've put this book together, and then you can take it from there.

A worship service or a special occasion such as a wedding or a baptism is often the entry point to a congregation for may people. So, after I make some introductions, I start with two chapters, "Sunday morning," and "Doing the rite thing." These will help you to understand how we worship and why we worship the way we do.

Then I think you should know what goes on in our congregations the rest of the week. So the next chapter is very cleverly titled, "What happens the rest of the week."

By this time in the book you will have begun to realize that what Lutherans believe plays a very big part in the way we do everything. That's why the next chapter talks about, "What we believe."

I move on to talk about some practical concerns about living as a Christian in "What we do with what we've got." Then come some ideas about how we talk with other people about our faith in "Sharing the good news."

"Living what we believe," explains some of the ELCIC's positions on things like gambling and sex and censorship. The next chapter, "Pastors, preachers, and other creatures," will help you to understand the role our ministers play in the life of the ELCIC.

I put two chapters of background material near the back for convenient reference. "All in the family" will tell you about Martin Luther and also about another group of Canadian Lutherans called the Lutheran Church—Canada. A chapter follows that explains how the ELCIC works.

Just before my short final chapter, you will find a dictionary called "Learning to speak Lutheran." While you're reading, if you find a word that may not be familiar, I have tried to anticipate that and to give a simple explanation in my dictionary.

Finally, at the very, very back, I have written a few words that I hope you will save until you finish reading the rest of the book. This is not a mystery novel. You don't have to look back there to see how things turn out. However, I did write those words with the hope that you would have read the rest of the book first.

Happy reading. I hope you enjoy this book as much as I did writing it.

Your brother in Christ,
Kenn Ward

Chapter 1

Photo: Kenn Ward

Hi there!

The Evangelical Lutheran Church in Canada is quite a mouthful, and it is hardly a household name. Some of our own members can't get the name straight. Whenever Canadian churches are mentioned, people are more likely to talk about the Roman Catholics or the United Church or the Anglicans or the Baptists or the Presbyterians.

Even the *Globe and Mail* gets confused about who we are. In one story in Canada's national newspaper, a list of Canadian churches appeared with a comma stuck right in the middle of our name: Evangelical, Lutheran.

This book will help interested or curious people learn something about us. People who are thinking about becoming members of the Evangelical Lutheran

Church in Canada or people who are already members but who want to learn more about our church will want to read it.

Incidentally, instead of using the term "the Evangelical Lutheran Church in Canada" all the way through this book, I'm going to call it "the ELCIC," since this is the handle most of us use most of the time.

From sea to sea to sea

Part of the reason that we aren't very well known is that there aren't very many of us in Canada. Most Canadians know how big Skydome is even if they've only seen a news clip of a Toronto Blue Jays baseball game. All the active Lutherans in Canada would fill Skydome about five or six times.

Lutherans, active and inactive, form about 2.4% of the population of Canada. The 1991 census reported that there were 636,505 of us. The ELCIC claims loyalty from about 206,000 of these.

The ELCIC is a young denomination. It was created in 1986 by the merger of the Evangelical Lutheran Church **of** Canada (note the "of"), and the Lutheran Church in America—Canada Section.

We inhabit the land from sea to sea to sea. There were a few of us in Newfoundland for a time, but most of us moved on and the congregation disbanded. We have never become established in Prince Edward Island. However, you will find a bunch of us around Halifax and in Lunenburg County on Nova Scotia's South Shore. There is a sprinkling of us in New Brunswick if you look carefully.

If you travel up the St. Lawrence, you will find us in Montreal, along the Seaway in Ontario and on into Toronto and its many surrounding communities. Branch up the Ottawa River and we make up a significant part of the population of the Ottawa Valley, as we also do in Southwestern Ontario, especially around Kitchener-Waterloo.

Head north and we thin out again through Northern Ontario, but we are there. Out on the Prairies, we are an important part of the geography, particularly in major cities such as Winnipeg, Regina, Saskatoon, Calgary, and Edmonton. Camrose, Alberta, is also an important place on the Lutheran map.

Cross the Rockies into British Columbia and you will rub shoulders with us in Vancouver and Victoria as well as in the province's prosperous valleys. A few of us have even ventured into Whitehorse in the Yukon and Yellowknife in the Northwest Territories.

We are your friends and neighbors, but we are often a bit shy about talking about our faith so you may not know that we attend a Lutheran church.

Martin Luther

We call ourselves Lutherans because we base our beliefs on the teachings of Martin Luther, an Augustinian priest whose ideas got him in trouble with the Roman Catholic Church in the 16th century. I'll tell you a lot more about him in the chapter called "All in the family."

Luther hated the idea that a denomination would name itself after him. He wasn't trying to start a denomination; he was trying to reform the church. Luther questioned what the church of his time was doing. Eventually, the Roman Catholic Church expelled Luther and those who followed him as heretics.

That rift is only now beginning to heal. Both sides said many things that we now regret. In the past few decades, Lutherans and Roman Catholics and other Christians have been talking with each other. We have learned that we have a lot in common and that what we share is more important than the things that we disagree about.

That word "evangelical"

Some of us are a bit uncomfortable with that word "evangelical" in our name, even though it is a very good Lutheran word.

And I suspect that many people feel that same discomfort when they hear us use that word evangelical as we introduce ourselves. ("Did he say evangelical?"

they inwardly gasp or groan as they desperately search for an excuse to rush away as quickly as they can.)

Before we go any further into this book, I need to tell you that nobody is suddenly going to jump out from between the pages and ask if you have been saved.

In North America, the term evangelical has become identified with fundamentalist Christians. We are not part of that crowd. Although there are aspects of their faith that enrich all of Christianity, they also teach some things that we strongly disagree with.

Evangelical is a word deeply rooted in our history. It means "those who share good (or God's) news." Notice the word "angel" in the middle.

Evangelical was the name that was used as far back as the 1520s. It describes the church that organized around the teachings of Martin Luther with the gospel as the center of those teachings.

This evangelical church summed up its beliefs in a statement of basic principles that are called "confessions." I'll explain more about those basic beliefs in the chapter "What we believe."

If you stick with me that far, you'll discover some things about Christianity that may surprise you. If you thought that being a Christian was all about a lot of don't-do-this and don't-do-that kind of rule keeping, you'll find that Lutherans have a different idea.

But before we get there, we need to get better acquainted.

Introductions

Let me introduce myself to you.

I am one of those people who sometimes wear their collars backwards. At the moment, I am the editor of the ELCIC's national magazine *Canada Lutheran*. Before serving in that position, I was a parish pastor for 18 years. I am also a lifelong Lutheran, so you'll have to excuse my obvious bias.

I am very proud of being a Lutheran. We are justifiably proud of our long heritage. But my main source of pride is the wonderful people who have been my Christian sisters and brothers in this very special family of believers that God brought into being through our baptisms.

I don't remember my baptism. I was a baby. My mom was Lutheran and my dad was Anglican. I was baptized on Sunday, August 26, 1946, at my parents' home by a Lutheran minister, Dr. Clifford S. Roberts from St. John's Lutheran Church in Waterloo, Ontario.

I heard a pastor once say that we should memorize the date of our baptism and celebrate it as we do our birthday. I was very impressed by the idea. I was so impressed that I persuaded my wife that we should do just that, and each August 26 we do.

However, that happens because she remembers such details, not me. In fact, I had to get the date from her so I could write it down here. Hey, I need all the help I can get from my family! That's why I'm so grateful that God added all those people to my family tree when I was baptized.

Incidentally, my wife, Diane, was a member of the United Church of Canada before we were married. She decided that it would look strange if the Lutheran minister's wife attended a different church so she became a Lutheran.

I think she's glad she did, even though she still claims some things don't sit quite right in her United Church bones. Every now and then we both enjoy worshiping in the church where she grew up. It's also the church where we were married by a Lutheran pastor and a United Church minister, just to convince everyone that we were doing it right and proper.

You have probably figured out from my name that I like to be a bit unorthodox. "Kenn" came from a dare made during lunch in high school. A couple of friends said that I wouldn't dare write it down on a paper that was due, and if I did, the teachers would never accept it. Wrong! Somehow it's stuck with me ever since.

I was baptized "Kenneth John James" using the names of the landlord's son, my grandfather and my godfather respectively. My earliest memory of church is that of my mother taking me to Sunday school on my birthday when I was quite young. The teacher made me feel right at home, and I've been going ever since.

I can't spin you any tale about a memorable conversion experience. I grew up in the church, and I'm still growing (in more ways than my waistline, I hope). Along the way God has placed a number of people in my path who have challenged and enriched my faith.

Certainly I've had dry times when I have had some pretty strong doubts about this whole church and God business. By God's grace and mercy, I'm still hanging in there.

Learning to speak Lutheran

By the way, we Lutherans use many code words. When we use them, we sometimes forget that other people might not have a clue what we are talking about. Whenever I used such a word, I added it to a special list in the chapter at the back of the book called, "Learning to speak Lutheran."

A language problem

Our language problem has been more than a few words that need definition. Until recently, many of us spoke neither of Canada's official languages as our mother tongue. We have been a church of immigrants who were busy learning the language. When we attended church we often used the language we brought with us because it was more comfortable for us to worship God that way. Hearing about God's love in words we understood made us feel more at home in a strange land.

In some of our churches, we still use the languages we brought with us—Danish, Estonian, Finnish, Icelandic, German, Latvian, Lithuanian, Norwegian, Swedish. We are also reaching out to other newcomers and so we sometimes use Spanish, the major Chinese dialects, and Vietnamese. We'll probably add a few more along the way. In Montreal we've begun to use French. However, most of our churches use English. (Even though a few of the words I have sometimes used in my sermons might cause people to question that statement.)

I have to share a story one of our bishops told me. It's just one of many I'm going to tell you in the hope they will help you get to know us better.

(Our bishops got a bit paranoid when they heard that I was writing a book and would be quoting some of them from time to time. Don't worry, bishop. I won't mention your name, and I've changed the story enough to keep people from guessing which bishop told me what.)

This bishop said that when he visited a Finnish congregation in his synod, the people had a hard time talking with him in English. Except when he started to talk about the mortgage on their building. Suddenly, they all spoke perfect English.

Changing collars

The Lutheran church has changed a lot from Luther's day. We were once a persecuted minority protected by a few rebel rulers. Lutherans are now the state church in Scandinavian countries. We also play a prominent role in a number of other countries, especially Germany and the United States of America.

While we are few in numbers in Canada, Lutherans are one of the largest denominations in the world. Until the middle of this century, we operated pretty much on our own in each country without paying much attention to what Lutherans were doing in other countries. However, most of us now belong to the Lutheran World Federation. Although this helps us to keep in touch with each other, we still each make our own decisions about how we will live out our Lutheranism.

When we first came to this country we were mostly farmers and factory workers and clerks and laborers. We were a blue-collar crowd.

Now most of us are part of Canada's middle class, and we are upwardly mobile. As we began to have opportunities for education, many of us put away our blue collars and joined the white-collar crowd. This is changing us and not all the changes are necessarily for the better.

14

The white-collar crowd bring a different way of looking at and doing things. Some of our traditional members no longer feel at home. As a result, we may be in danger of losing the very people who have been the supporting force behind this church for so many years.

My family is typical. My mom and dad, both very bright people, received public school educations because of limited choices. My brother and I and our wives are university graduates, and our sister, who is a high school graduate, is no slouch in the brains department either.

None of my family live in the blue-collar neighborhoods where we grew up. My mother and sister share a comfortable apartment, and my brother and I have homes in middle-class neighborhoods.

For many years we followed our members to the new suburbs, and as they built houses for their families, we built houses of worship for them to attend. We still do that today.

We are beginning to take another look at those neighborhoods where we grew up. A few of us still go to the churches that we originally built in those neighborhoods. Some are finding ways to invite the new people who have moved there to be part of their congregations.

Some ground rules

Still with me? Good.

By now you've probably realized that this isn't going to be a very "churchy" book in the traditional sense. When my friend Jim Taylor from Wood Lake Books asked me to write this book, he told me that he wanted something along the lines Ralph Milton followed when he wrote *This United Church of Ours*. I interpreted that to mean that I was to write a somewhat irreverent but affectionate account that would help people to learn about the Evangelical Lutheran Church in Canada.

Incidentally, Jim is also one of the people who talked me into applying for the position of editor of *Canada Lutheran*. I had objected that I liked being a parish pastor. Jim quoted the former editor of the

United Church Observer, A. C. Forrest, who once told him that a church magazine makes a good pulpit. The whole church becomes your parish. You can tell that Jim is a very persuasive person. I'm writing this book, aren't I?

The folks at Wood Lake have set a style that takes religious stuff and explains it in the kind of language most people use. Jim told me that I should write as if I was trying to explain things to a good friend. So, for the most part, that's the way this book will be.

Friends accept each other just as they are. They share the good and the bad as it comes along. I hope you'll take me that way, too—even my corny attempts at humor.

I'll try to be very honest with you and tell it like it is, or at least the way I see it. I've asked several people with experience in the particular areas I'm talking about to review what I've written. These are people whose judgment I trust and who have helped to keep things as accurate as possible.

Ultimately, however, this book is one person's account of the ELCIC—mine. I hope that it will get you thinking, talking, and acting.

Thinking, talking, and acting

That's right. I expect you to do more than sit there and read this stuff. You might toss my book in the trash before you finish it. At least I'll have gotten some action out of you. I really hope that what I have to say will make a positive difference in your life.

I didn't take on this project because it would bring me fame and fortune. Jim Taylor claims I'm already famous enough. Or was that infamous? And the royalties he promised aren't worth discussing. I certainly won't be able to give up my day job.

I hope that you will discover, as I have, that the ELCIC is a group of people with whom you can grow in grace and faith.

Faith involves the whole person. One of my favorite verses in the Bible is where Jesus said, "You shall love the Lord your God with all your heart, and with all your soul, and with all your mind." (Matthew 22:37) Did you notice the word "mind" in that verse?

Faith does not mean parking your brains at the door. As one person noted, we are called to be transformed by the **renewal** of our minds, not by their **removal**. I get really annoyed with intelligent people who suddenly start to babble pious platitudes because they think it sounds religious.

There is enough woolly-headed muddle in the church passing itself off as profound and churchly piety without you and me adding to that mess. God gave us minds. Let's use them.

God also gave us tongues. We must use them too. I know, I know. Your tongue can get you into trouble. I've said many things in my time that would have been better left unsaid.

However, silence is not golden; it can be deadly. The ELCIC is not a perfect church. This is not a perfect world. If we keep silent about the things that need to be changed or improved, how are people ever going to get around to changing those things?

Ignorance is not bliss; it is an excuse for not having to do anything. That brings me to doing.

One thing I've noticed about the ELCIC is that we like to talk, even if some of us don't put much thought into the words that trip off our tongues. We also have some people who bless us with words of wisdom.

Many times, however, we just talk. Sometimes this is called "consciousness raising." That's a 60s term that seems to mean that, if enough people get the right vibes, the problem will somehow dissolve in a haze of warm fuzzy feelings. Sometimes we run the risk of getting lost in such a haze.

Perhaps you will be one of those rare gems who come our way now and then, who not only are willing to think and talk, but also to act. I am always amazed by what God can do with a little faith.

Chapter 2

Photo: Neil Thomsen

Sunday Morning

Many people's first introduction to the Lutheran church is through a worship service. So let's start there.

You will likely receive a sincere, though sometimes shy, greeting at the door. Someone will probably hand you a worship guide (which we call a bulletin). You will discover a bewildering set of instructions inside— sometimes referring to several different books, bulletin inserts, page numbers and hymn numbers.

At first, a person going to a Lutheran worship service can feel a bit like a one-handed paper hanger who attended a jugglers' convention. You know that you can do it, but for a while you feel a bit out of place.

Getting used to our way of worship takes some time and practice. At first things may seem very foreign and unfamiliar. Those who take the time learn that it can be a rewarding experience, especially if you make it a regular and routine part of your life.

More than one person, caught in a moment of crisis, has discovered that the familiar routine and words, learned and remembered through repetition, have brought comfort and healing.

Participation

If you plan to go to a Lutheran church expecting to sit there and be entertained, you'd better beat a hasty retreat. Our worship is not meant for spectators.

Our style of worship works best when everyone gets involved: standing up, sitting down, perhaps kneeling, shaking hands, walking up to the front, eating, drinking, singing, speaking, praying, maybe even laughing and crying!

That last part may surprise you if you thought that Lutheran worship was very stiff and formal. At many of our services, there is a very specific order to the way things are done because we like to have things done properly and in good order. But the service is only as stiff and formal as the people worshiping or leading worship demand it to be or allow it to become.

This thing called "liturgy"

We call our style of worship "liturgy." Liturgy is a Greek word that means "the work of the people." Lutheran worship can seem like very hard work until you begin to understand how to make it work for you. Then it becomes rewarding.

Lutheran worship usually follows a pattern that has evolved over centuries of use. We call this pattern a liturgical order. A number of the songs and sayings are English translations of words that Christians have used for a very long time. Some of them go way back to the earliest days of the Christian Church, and some are found in the Bible.

If you happen to drop by an Anglican or Roman Catholic church during worship, you will find that much of what they do looks and sounds a lot like what we Lutherans do. The order may be a bit different, and they may use a few different tunes, but we all use much of the same basic liturgies to guide our worship lives.

Our congregations do liturgy in a wide variety of ways. Some follow the book quite closely and allow very little room for change or experiment. Others fill their worship with all sorts of innovations and an equal assortment of musical instruments.

Whatever style of worship is used in the Lutheran congregation which you choose, it likely reflects the moods, needs, and history of that congregation. So treat it with respect. The service is an important way for that group of believers to share their faith and to help you grow in faith with them.

Life among the fossils

If the liturgy that Lutherans use is so old, how, you may wonder, can it still appeal to modern people? I confess that there are times when the way we worship feels as if we are dragging around a pile of fossils. That's not because the service is deader than the dinosaurs, but because the people worshiping with it sometimes seem headed the way of the dinosaur.

This happens when a congregation lets its worship get stale. Frankly, such behavior annoys and bewilders me.

People would be quick to replace the communion bread if it started to grow moldy, and they would pour out the wine if it began to turn to vinegar. They wouldn't let water sit in the baptismal font until it got stagnant.

It takes imagination and vigilance to keep our rich liturgical heritage from becoming a museum piece. The words and music of a service can get tired and tattered—along with those who use them—unless the worshipers work at keeping them fresh and vigorous.

Yes, there are worship services where both my mind and my bottom grow numb. I've been so bored that I thought watching paint peel would be more interesting. As a matter of fact, there have been a couple of paint

20

chips I grew to know rather well.

I'm glad that these dull moments haven't caused me to give up on worship. The good times more than make up for those bad times. Even in the dullest service, there is often some spark that kindles a bit of hope or joy or determination in me.

Waking up

One Sunday while my family and I were on vacation, we decided that we would drag ourselves off to worship. At least I was dragging. I don't remember why I was so tired that morning, but I was really, really tired. If I had been any more tired, that service could have been a funeral service for me—and I wouldn't have noticed the difference.

The service that Sunday was lead by a seminary student. (Someone once said that Lutherans don't have to go to purgatory because they have to listen to sermons by seminarians.) This kid was nervous, and he was very, very inexperienced. He messed up parts of the service that I didn't believe could be messed up. And his sermon! Snore time!

But he was trying to do his best. It may have been the simple sincerity behind his struggling words. Or the words of a familiar hymn that we sang (not very well as I recall). Or something mentioned (or perhaps mumbled) in one of the prayers. I'm not sure.

What I do remember is that as the service moved along, I began to feel myself waking up. Gradually I became invigorated and enthusiastic about being alive. Somehow, the spirit of God breathed freshness into my weary soul. I realized that just being among the faithful people of God at worship can restore one's faith, even with a poor preacher and a service that somehow muddles its way through to the end of the hour.

Liturgical two-step

Lutherans do like to have their worship done properly, but a person can overdo this proper thing. I once conducted a service where I was supposed to demon-

21

strate the right way to do things. The intention was that what I did would be copied by other pastors when they went back home. I had been a pastor for several years and thought I knew what to do. However, the instructions for that particular service were so complicated that another pastor stood at the back and, whenever I got confused, gave me hand signals for what to do next.

It was one of the more memorable services I have attended for none of the right reasons. I was a nervous wreck. I have seldom been so miserable in my life. I felt like a puppet on a string rather than a child of God celebrating the good gifts of our gracious God.

I left that service vowing to remember the basics and not to sweat the small stuff. It's worked out very well.

Our focus should be on praising God and not on worrying so much about how to hold our hands and bob our heads. If the liturgical dance causes people to shuffle out the door, then we have served neither God nor our brothers and sisters in Christ.

Managing the muddle

Even those of us who have been doing the Lutheran thing since birth find it hard to get the hang of things the first time that we go to another Lutheran church. When do you stand up or sit down? In some churches, there are also times when you are expected to kneel.

The easiest way I know is to find a seat near the back (if the faithful haven't already filled them). It's something like going to a formal dinner and trying to figure out which knife or fork or spoon to use. Just watch the others and copy them. After a while you'll find that things begin to make sense. With a little practice you are soon up and down right in time with the rest of them.

Many congregations provide a printed folder that includes a set of instructions for the worship service. The people who write these bulletins often forget those who have never worshiped there before. So it pays to allow yourself enough time to read it over.

Even after all these years as a Lutheran and as a

pastor, I still try to get to worship early so that I can study the instructions for the service beforehand. I refold the bulletin inside out. This way the bulletin becomes a handy bookmark which I place at the page that is being used. It also allows me to check out the order of service at a glance.

You need a least one bookmark, even if you just use a finger to hold your place. You will find that the congregation jumps to other parts of the book and to other pieces of paper, sometimes even to other books, and then suddenly jumps back to where you were a few minutes ago without anyone announcing what page they are on. If you don't have the starting point marked, by the time you find that page, they've moved ahead a page or two and then...

Some tips

It's really not as hard as it sounds, but it does take some getting used to.

When in doubt, leave it out. If you can't find the page or the paper, don't worry about it. Just relax and listen. You'll get more out of that than sweating about a minor miss.

Better yet, quietly ask someone near you for a bit of help. Most members gladly lend a hand. This first step can be a good way to break the ice and begin to meet people in a congregation. Often, longtime members are just as shy and nervous about saying something to a newcomer as the newcomer is about speaking to someone in that crowd of strangers.

Changing the book

Lutheran worship books are something like cars. Every few years, we come up with a different model. I've lived through the "black book," the "red book," and now we have the "green book" (*Lutheran Book of Worship*). There is already talk about a new book being developed for use early in the next century. (Someone asked if this one was going to be the "plaid book"!)

The Lutheran congregation which you attend may

have several worship supplements along with the *Lutheran Book of Worship* or even in place of it. Remember we believe in evangelical freedom. Lutheran worship not only reflects a rich tradition, it should also reflect the lives and the times of the people who are worshiping.

Our basic rule of thumb is that things be done properly with good order. Sounds a bit like the Canadian constitution, doesn't it? Things may be in a bit of a muddle, but we try to keep up the appearance that everything is peaceful and calm. Strangely enough, there are times when appearances may not be all that deceiving.

Lutheran Book of Worship

Since the *Lutheran Book of Worship* (which many of us call "the green book") is the standard worship resource for most of our congregations, it helps to understand how it works. This is a book that you can't judge by its cover because it is really two books bound together.

The first part has a variety of worship services along with several other printed worship resources such as prayers and psalms. This part has "page" numbers. So if you see a page listed or hear a page announced, start looking in the front of the book.

However, if you see a "hymn" listed or hear a hymn announced, head for the back of the book. This part is the hymn section. The only tricky part is that the first few hymns are called "canticles." These are not used very often. Most worship leaders will give you plenty of instructions when a canticle is used so don't worry about them.

If you take time to browse through the *Lutheran Book of Worship*, you will discover a rich treasure house. There is a lot of good stuff packed between those green covers. This book is not only for public worship. Those pages can help shape your faith in private moments too. In fact, some of the more devout Lutherans know and treasure their worship book almost as much as they do their Bibles.

A word about reading the Word

Speaking of Bibles... The Bible is a very basic part of our worship. Some congregations may even have a Bible for your use as one of the worship books. In any case, the Bible is quoted and used in the service even when worshipers don't have copies.

If you don't know your way around the Bible, nothing is more embarrassing than sitting in a group who flick back and forth between all those chapters and verses while you're still trying to figure out if you should be looking in the back part or the front part.

The front part is called "The Old Testament." This talks about the things that happened before Jesus came on the scene. The back part is called "The New Testament." This talks about Jesus as well as the things that happened in the early Christian Church.

With practice you begin to know where the different books of the Bible are. Every Bible has an index that lists the page number for each book. Even experienced Christians sometimes have to use the index, or they hunt around to find things.

Every book in the Bible is numbered by chapter and verse to help people find things easily. Here is how the code works. Say you were asked to look up "1 Corinthians 3:12." "Corinthians" is the name of the book. If there is a number in front of the name, such as "1," then you know that there is more than one book in the Bible with that name.

In the version of the Bible that I am using, 1 Corinthians begins on page 165. The problem with this particular version is that page 165 is found in two different places. That's because they started numbering all over again when they got to The New Testament.

Now I need to find the chapter and verse: "3:12" means chapter 3, verse 12. That's the shorthand way we use to write the information. Have a good read!

Who leads?

As you might expect, the pastor leads the worship service. However, the pastor is not the only person who should be up there leading. There are a lot of leadership opportunities for laypeople too.

Some congregations have problems with letting laypeople lead part of the service. Some object that they aren't "holy" enough to do it. If being "holy" enough is the standard, then we'd better stop those sinning saints (or is it saintly sinners?) whom we call pastors from leading us too.

Once in a while someone says, "I thought that's what we paid the pastor for." Such thinking not only shortchanges all that a pastor does in a congregation, it also keeps many talented people from using their God-given gifts in a way which helps the congregation give God richer praise. The liturgy is "the work of the people" not just the work of the pastor. (Remember, that's what the word "liturgy" literally means!)

While preaching and presiding at Communion are reserved for the pastor, there are all sorts of opportunities for laypeople to lead in worship—they can serve as cantors or readers, or they can lead the prayers or help to serve Communion.

The basic order

There are three basic parts to most of our services: confession of sin, proclamation of the Word, and celebration of the Sacrament of Holy Communion. Sometimes this is reduced to proclamation of the Word, but this practice is falling out of favor.

Perhaps the easiest way to remember how the basic pattern works is to think about a family gathering with people eating together and sharing stories. We are God's family gathered together to share family stories and the family meal.

What I am going to say is only a basic guide, but it should help you to understand the logic behind most Lutheran services.

Yes, you must confess

To be strictly accurate, confession is not part of the service. It is sort of a service to get ready for the service—

kind of like brushing your teeth and combing your hair before you go out in public.

The idea of confession upsets some people. They claim that this shoves sin down people's throats when we should be telling them the good news about God's love.

I have bad news for such good-news folks. Sin is a terrible reality in our world and in our lives. There are many times when I would like to forget that I have sinned against God in thought, word, and deed, and that I have not loved my neighbor as myself. Confession helps me to remember that I'm not quite as great a guy as I would like to believe I am.

We are simultaneously both saint and sinner. (I'll explain this idea in the chapter "What we believe.") Something must be done about that sin. Otherwise we live as though we were trying to ignore a sewer that is building up gas. You have to wake up and smell the sewer gas before the fumes slowly choke you to death. Then you have to release the pressure or the whole thing will blow sky high and take you with it.

I don't think that we need to treat confession as groveling before God. It is a healthy reminder of who is really in charge and of how badly we manage things when we pretend that we own the place. Luther said that we should renew our baptism every day by getting our lives with God and each other sorted out and cleaned up on a daily basis.

In some congregations the baptismal font is the focal point for this part of the service. As people focus on the font and confess their sin, the font reminds us that our sins are washed away in the waters of Baptism. No matter how grimy we get, God's grace will not let any of that dirt stick to us.

Sharing the Word

Now we come to the first part of the service after confession, if it has been used. This is when we tell family stories as we share and celebrate around the Word of God.

Every Sunday has a different theme. The Prayer of

the Day and the Bible lessons for this day reflect that theme. There are usually three lessons: normally one from the Old Testament, a lesson from one of the four Gospels, and a lesson from the rest of the New Testament. (There are some variations in this pattern but this is the norm most of the time.)

Sometimes the hymns and the sermon will also pick up on the theme. This depends on the priorities that are at work in a congregation at the time.

I like the discipline of working through a set of Bible lessons that have been specifically assigned for use at each of our services. During the time I served as a parish pastor, this helped to keep me from riding my hobby horses every Sunday. Still, canny pastors can gallop through more than one service riding their trusty steeds.

When I served in the parish, a lot of prayer went into the sermons I preached. There are times when I still pray a lot through this part of the service, especially when I'm not the preacher. We preachers need all the help and encouragement we can get.

Sometimes nothing in the sermon seems to get through to me. At times like that I pray that some glimmer of insight or encouragement will reach the other listeners and me, that the Holy Spirit will speak to us.

Preaching is hard work. Most of us tend to be very hard on our preachers at least some of the time, although seldom as hard as they are on themselves. Much of the criticism of preachers is not really fair, particularly if you try to compare your overworked pastor with that television preacher who looks so great and sounds so wonderful.

You could smile right into the camera like that too if you had someone to do your make up and help you to research and write the sermon that you read from the teleprompter just the way your director told you to do it at rehearsal.

I'm not trying to make excuses for lazy pastors who don't do their homework and who never practise what they are going to preach. We have the right to expect our pastors to pack their best efforts into those words of instruction and inspiration. That's why we sit in the pew while they stand in the pulpit.

I look at it this way. As a baseball fan, I know that a batter who is hitting .300 is having a good season. Think about that. We cheer for a fellow who, for 70 percent of the time, is not doing the job he is paid for. No one thinks there is anything strange about that. After all, a baseball player can't hit a home run or even a base hit every time he steps up to the plate. It is not humanly possible.

Your pastor isn't going to hit a homer every time she or he steps into the pulpit either. Just think of how many different people with so many different things going on in their lives are sitting there listening to that sermon. If the pastor's words speak to me, they may have very little to say to you that Sunday.

I try to find something worthwhile to hold on to from each sermon. Every so often the pastor's words get me right where I live.

The rest of the time I'm a bit like the lady who always found something encouraging to say to the pastor after every service. After a particularly bad sermon one Sunday, she shook his hand and said, "You picked nice hymns today."

Celebrating Communion

Now we get to the altar call. I love to say things like that, and then watch faithful Lutherans sneak a peek at the nearest exit.

Before you check out on me, think about the purpose of an altar call. People who respond to an altar call have realized their need for God and stand up in front of everyone to admit that need.

That moment changes some people's lives forever. In an evangelistic meeting, those people are prayed over and sent on their way with a promise of future support in their decision. Sometimes there is good follow-through. Sometimes not. When there is not, it seems that the decision was made on the basis of emotional hype. When the emotional high goes away, so does the decision.

Once in a while, the Lutheran altar call that I'm talking about can be a real high. More often than not, it's an ordinary event that comes in the midst of the highs and lows of our everyday lives. We also march right up to the front of the church, freely admitting our need of God—our hunger and thirst for God's love and forgiveness—out in the open where everyone can see us.

Jesus meets us there in words of hope and promise: "The body of Christ given for you. The blood of Christ shed for you." Those words "for you" mean just that, whether you are burdened, celebrating, struggling, worried, hopeful, troubled, timid or feeling great. And Christ's presence in this sacrament is as real as the bread we chew and the wine we sip.

Holy Communion is the family meal. In one congregation that I served, we would sometimes set up the worship space with tables and tablecloths, plates and cups and knives and forks and all the rest. Then we would sit down to worship. When we got to the part of the service where we celebrated Communion, we would share the bread and the wine with each other and then continue with a regular church dinner.

I prefer to have the whole service complete with Holy Communion every Sunday. Otherwise I feel as if we have set the table for the meal and then leave without eating it. I need assurance and reminders of God's love every day, not just on a scheduled Sunday or two. So I'm glad that more and more Lutheran congregations are making Holy Communion part of their regular pattern of worship.

The Church Year

The theme for a particular service on a particular Sunday depends on the time of year when that service is held. I'm not talking about the date on the calendar. Christians have their own Church Year that doesn't match the calendar year.

In the Church Year, there are three seasons— Christmas, Easter, and Pentecost. Unfortunately, it gets a bit more complicated than that. (I'm not going to explain each of the terms here. You can find those definitions in the chapter called "Learning to speak Lutheran.")

The Christmas cycle begins with Advent. Simply count back four Sundays from December 25 and you reach the beginning of Advent and the start of the Church Year. Christmas itself isn't over when the stores stop playing Christmas music. We keep on celebrating until January 6, the Epiphany. After that we count the Sundays as Sundays-after-the-Epiphany until we reach Lent.

Lent begins the Easter cycle. There are six Sundays in Lent, which is started by counting back from Easter Sunday. The date for Easter is figured out with a complicated formula that none of us can figure out. We find the information on a chart in the front of the little appointment book that Lutheran pastors get every year from Augsburg Fortress, Canada, the ELCIC's bookstore.

The last week in Lent is called Holy Week, and it includes Maundy Thursday and Good Friday. In some congregations, Easter Vigil, which happens on Saturday night, is also added. The addition of Easter Vigil creates a special worship package that has parts on each of the three days. This worship "package" is called the Triduum. (I know, I know. Where did we get such strange names? Tradition.)

Then comes Easter. We think that Easter is so great that we celebrate it over seven Sundays. (Just to confuse things, we also sometimes talk about every Sunday as being a little Easter. This is because Jesus rose from the dead on a Sunday morning.)

Finally, we reach Pentecost Sunday. For the rest of the year we number each Sunday after Pentecost, unless the fixed date for a special festival falls on a Sunday. Finally, we reach the last Sunday in the Church Year which is called "Christ the King." Some congregations totally ignore these special festivals, while others jump on them as a chance to get away from routine, especially by the time they get to the 23rd Sunday after Pentecost.

Using the Lutheran coloring book

We have another wrinkle in our worship. We use different colors to remind ourselves of the time of the year, just the way winter has white snow and spring has green grass. You will see these colors used in a variety of ways in worship. This depends on how much the congregation uses visual expression to add another dimension of inspiration to its worship life.

Advent uses blue as a symbol of hope. White is a color that suggests brightness, light, and joy. It is used for festivals of Christ such as Christmas, the Epiphany, and Easter. The traditional color of Lent is purple. It suggests a somber time. Red or scarlet is the color of blood and of fire. It is used during Holy Week and on Pentecost Sunday as well as that special Lutheran festival, Reformation Sunday.

At other times, we use the color green as a symbol of growth. Still, I have to confess that, when I was a youngster, I thought we used green because we had run out of imagination.

Facing the music

I don't know what your favorite music might be. I like just about every kind of music myself (even if my staff and my family won't let me play my Stompin' Tom Connors tapes when they are around).

Most Lutheran congregations use an organ or a piano to pump out their tunes. Those tunes tend to be classical or from tried and true traditions, some going back over a thousand years. There is no reason why we have to stick to this kind of music, but it has worn well over the years while many fads have come and gone.

There are no rules that forbid the use of any musical instrument in our services. At one time or another, I've heard most of them used at worship. All we ask is that the musician play well and for the glory of God.

I've been to Lutheran services that used rock, jazz, folk, rap and pop. I have some friends I'm trying to talk into doing a country-western version of the liturgy, and I know that there is a polka version around somewhere.

Over time the best of these will become part of our tradition and the trite stuff will fade away.

Whither the future?

My family and I recently watched a video tape of the Danish comedian and musician, Victor Borge. Our teenage children find him as funny as I did when I was their age, as did people who laughed along with him long before I was born. Suddenly my daughter asked, "Why are most of the people in the audience old?"

She might have been asking about far too many of our Sunday morning services. While there are encouraging signs of youth here and there in some of our congregations, far too many have become the place where grandma and grandpa go.

Part of it is a cultural thing. When it comes to Victor Borge, it's not cool for kids to admit that they get a kick out of an old guy who plays classical music and tells corny jokes. It's also not cool for kids in our culture to go to church.

That's sad because many cool kids are being left out in the cold.

I'm not convinced that changing the service to reflect the latest teen trend is the answer. As a pastor who had to do more than one service on a Sunday morning, there were many times when I was part of exactly the same service, with the same sermon, hymns and lessons, but with different people.

One service would bomb, and the next one would be great. One service would take your breath away, while the next would make you want to hold your nose. Same service. Different people.

Part of the answer involves making sure that our kids have the chance to be part of worship before peer pressure convinces them they shouldn't like that kind of stuff. It also helps to have parents who worship regularly, not out of habit, but because the Sunday service really is important to them. You can't kid the kids. They know the difference.

If you find a way to help them hang in there, let me

know. What I do know is that there were things about services that I didn't like when I first heard them. As a teen, I preferred the Beatles to Bach. I still like the Beatles, but Bach kind of grows on you with time.

Our way of worship has stood the test of many centuries. It has gradually changed and evolved over time to include the best of what has come along. I would like to believe that it will keep on doing that. That won't happen if our kids don't become part of the process.

Summing up

I hope that all this hasn't left you feeling the way I do after my friend Frank tries to explain cricket to me. I know that he loves the game and finds it very exciting, but he's never been able to get that enthusiasm to rub off on me. Fortunately, we both love the Blue Jays and baseball so perhaps it doesn't really matter.

But worship **does** matter. Worship is vital for a Christian if you want to continue to be a Christian. Most of the time worship is something you have to do with other people. Why do you think that Jesus taught us to pray **our** Father?

Oh, the ocean or the mountains, the brooks and the trees and the flowers can all be inspiring, but none of them can tell you that God loves you like sharing worship with others can.

I love to worship in the Lutheran way. I freely admit that I am very biased about this. It's been a major part of my life for much of my life. But, when you have a good thing going for you, why wouldn't you want other people to be part of it?

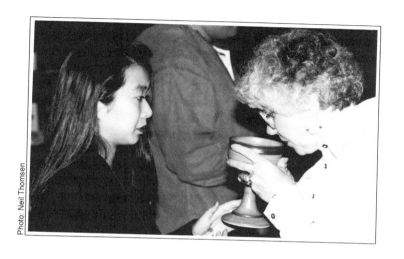

Chapter 3

Photo: Neil Thomsen

Doing the rite thing

When I served a parish in Toronto, we sometimes talked about the CNE Christians. We weren't talking about people who went to the Canadian National Exhibition. We meant those who only came on Christmas and Easter. Sometimes we also talked about these people as the ones who turned up whenever they wanted the church to recognize their hatching, matching, and dispatching.

There's a bit of bite to that churchy humor and a bit of sadness too. One feels like the parents who were told by a childless couple that they wished they could rent some kids for major holidays like Christmas. "Christmas," they said, "just doesn't seem like Christmas without children." That's nice. But they didn't really realize just how much they were missing.

There is a lot more to our ceremonies—our rites and our sacraments—than giving people a warm glow on significant occasions. However, I do want to stress that they do bring warmth and joy and many other good things to people's lives. That richness is appreciated more if worship is a regular, rather than an occasional, part of life.

Rites and sacraments

Over the centuries, Christians have called many things sacraments. However, Lutherans recognize only two sacraments—Holy Baptism and Holy Communion. There are other religious ceremonies or rites which are important to us too, such as marriage, but we don't call them sacraments.

To decide if something is a sacrament, we put it to a special test with three questions: Did Jesus tell us to do it? Does God use it to assure us of God's grace for us? Is there something very physical connected with it—an earthly element? For us, only Baptism and Communion pass the test.

We don't get too excited if other Christians want to call other things sacraments. The Bible doesn't even use the word sacrament.

I'm going to spend a bit of time telling you about our rites and sacraments in this chapter because these things usually raise many questions for people. I'll try to answer the questions I think most people have. You'll have to find out the rest for yourself. After a lifetime of learning, I'm still discovering new things about rites and sacraments myself.

Nothing but love

Grace is the word we use to talk about God's love. Grace is the most important word in the Lutheran vocabulary. Because God's grace is shared through these holy words and sacred ceremonies, we Lutherans sum up the core ministry of the church with the phrase "Word and Sacrament."

If we preach and teach the Word properly, then people will learn about God's grace. They will know how much God loves them. Realizing how much God loves you and learning to live in that love are the most important lessons a person can learn in life.

God also reaches out and touches us with grace in the sacraments. For us these are not quaint, ancient ceremonies that stir up distant memories. They give us a chance to share in things that are too deep for mere words.

In the celebration of Holy Baptism and Holy Communion, we are linked to the living, loving presence of God. We are assured that no matter how far we wander away from God's purpose for our lives, there is forgiveness for us. We are always welcome in God's place.

God's grace is as real as the water and the bread and the wine. In sacramental mystery, we join Jesus in his death and resurrection through the waters of baptism. Christ joins us, is really present with us, as we eat his holy meal.

Because we think that way, you can understand why we make such a big deal about these things being done properly. But no matter how big a deal we make of doing it right, in the end, grace is still a gift.

Baptism

Baptism is a very potent part of Christianity. It is part of the mystery of our relationship with God. In this simple ceremony, with a little water and a few ancient words about being baptized in the name of the Father and of the Son and of the Holy Spirit, we are made a part of the family of God—one holy catholic and apostolic Church—for all time and eternity. Awesome!

Baptism isn't like getting a flu shot. This isn't a sin shot which gives you immunization from sin. It is also not some kind of eternal fire insurance policy.

You're always welcome in God's family, but you can always choose to walk away. Baptism is a gift. Like any gift, it can be rejected.

God makes you part of the family for no other reason than sheer love. Baptism is a pure act of grace.

There is mystery in that, but it is not magic. In faith, we must lay claim to Baptism's promise.

Promises

Before we baptize adults, we ask them to spend some time being with other Christians. We hope that they might learn something about what being a Christian means. Then, if they really want to be part of the family, they may be baptized.

However, most Lutherans are baptized as babies. Someone has to teach them what it means to be part of the family; just as those babies are taught to walk and talk and all the other things babies must learn to grow into adulthood.

So we insist that parents promise to bring their children to worship regularly, and that they teach them how to pray and what it means to be a Christian. We are there to help them. We also expect the parents to help us to help them teach their children.

Unfortunately, some parents break their promises. One of the clues that usually tipped me off to pending trouble was when a new parent called and said that they wanted the baby "done." I knew that as soon as we "did" whatever it was the parents expected us to do, they would think that they were done too.

Bringing the baby for baptism is only the first step along the way. After you've made all those promises in front of God and the whole congregation, what are you going to do to keep them?

Parents who want their babies baptized need to think through their own lives with God. Do they really want that baby to follow in their footsteps?

Who decides?

It's very easy to agree to baptize a child when the pastor knows that the parents are active members of the congregation. But what do you do when you're pretty sure that the parents have seldom darkened the doorstep of any church?

More and more congregations insist that the parents become actively involved in the life of the congregation themselves before they will talk about baptizing baby. Otherwise it's like a stranger asking to be given a key to your house. They want to be treated like a member of the family without being part of the family and without intending to become part of the family.

A regular part of getting ready for any baptism is the time taken to teach about the basics of faith and the life of a Christian. In larger congregations, there may be regularly scheduled classes for adults preparing for baptism and for the parents of children who are being baptized. Because I served smaller congregations, I usually preferred to drop by the home of the people involved for a few visits to talk about what it all means.

The ELCIC is developing clearer procedures as well as teaching materials for what it calls the "adult catechumenate." Many people today have had little or no training in the Christian faith. They have never had a chance to find out what it means to be a church member. In the ELCIC's process, a person has the chance to become involved in the church through a special time of learning and friendship.

Sometimes people refuse to get involved with all this and then claim that the pastor refused to baptize their child. Fortunately, most people understand that we are taking their request seriously and are asking them to be just as serious about their responsibilities.

Suddenly a parent who hasn't read the Bible for years starts shopping around for Bible storybooks to read to their children and Bible story videos to add to the collection of cartoons and Disney movies. Bedtime and mealtime prayers are dusted off after being neglected for many years. It's no wonder many parents claim that having children helped them to rediscover the meaning of their own faith.

As we consider the right time to baptize, we need to be as gracious as the loving God in whose name we baptize. When our first-born son, Jed, died after an hour of life in this world, Diane and I took great comfort in knowing that a nurse had baptized him. We knew that God would have still loved him and cared for him even if that nurse hadn't baptized him. But at such moments, you aren't interested in theology.

Policies

An ordained pastor normally administers Baptism except in the case of an emergency. There are three types of people who may be baptized: children of members, children for whom other congregational members take the responsibility of nurturing their faith, and older children or adults who have received instruction, believe in Christ, and want to be baptized.

If you want to be baptized or to have a child baptized, you will likely have to decide about sponsors. A sponsor should be more than someone you pick to participate in the ceremony. You want that person to stand by the person being baptized throughout their spiritual journey. Sponsors are people who agree to take some responsibility for nurturing the faith of the person being baptized.

It is becoming increasingly common for the congregation in which the person is being baptized to pick someone from the congregation to be a sponsor. I like this idea because it shows that the congregation is taking responsibility for nurturing each person who is baptized in that congregation.

Parents may also pick sponsors and usually do. These people do not have to belong to the congregation or even be Lutheran. However, we assume that these people are involved in the faith and life of a Christian community because they are promising to help the baptized person learn and live the faith.

The baptismal ceremony

I was baptized in my parents' home on a Sunday afternoon. Although it was not unusual at the time, this would be unlikely to happen today. Baptism normally takes place at a service of the congregation.

People gather around the baptismal font. Each person to be baptized is presented. A prayer of thanksgiving is offered. The parents and sponsors are asked to renounce publicly sin and evil. (After all, we want to be sure the parents and sponsors know which side they are on.) Then everyone says the Apostles' Creed. These words have been used at baptisms by Christians to declare their faith, almost since the beginning of Christianity.

Water is poured or sprinkled over the person's head as the pastor baptizes the person in the name of the Father and of the Son and of the Holy Spirit. The pastor places both hands on the baptized person's head and prays that the gifts of the Holy Spirit will be poured upon the person being baptized.

The sign of a cross is traced on the forehead of the baptized, sometimes with special oil. Some Lutherans remember this moment in their baptisms by making the sign of the cross during worship when the Father, the Son, and the Holy Spirit are mentioned. There are small red crosses printed in the *Lutheran Book of Worship* to suggest times in the services when this might be done.

In some congregations a special white cape or poncho is placed over the newly baptized person. Other congregations present a special baptismal candle. These are meant to be baptismal souvenirs to help the people remember this important moment in their lives.

Finally, the newly baptized person is presented to the congregation and is welcomed by them into the family of God.

Every baptism is special, but some are particularly memorable. On one occasion, I baptized a father and his six children. We had seven members on the congregational council, and each one acted as a sponsor for a member of the family, while the mother, who was already baptized, watched proudly.

I was also deeply moved on the Sunday when I baptized the father of a teenage girl whom I had recently confirmed. He had asked his daughter to be his baptismal sponsor.

Affirmation of baptism

The *Lutheran Book of Worship* has a rite called

41

"Affirmation of Baptism." Many Lutherans find the term confusing because it includes "Confirmation" as one of its options.

At some point in the lives of people who have been baptized as babies, we hope that they will stand up in front of a congregation and personally lay claim to the promises of their baptisms. They will confirm that the faith in which they were baptized is their faith too. Lutherans call this "Confirmation."

However, there are more options in Affirmation of Baptism than Confirmation. Affirmation of Baptism can also be used as a ceremony to receive new members who were baptized in another Christian denomination and who are now joining a Lutheran congregation. A third use of this Affirmation is for members who have been inactive for a long time and who again want to take an active part in the life of the congregation.

We do not rebaptize people. We place the emphasis on what God does for us rather than on what we do. Baptism is God's gift of grace. With that viewpoint, it is impossible for us to say that God didn't get it right the first time.

By the way, when you are baptized, you become part of the Christian Church universal; the denomination where the baptizing was done is incidental to us and to most denominations. However, you should realize that when a person is baptized in a Lutheran congregation, the person also becomes a member of that congregation through that baptism.

A friend of mine is the pastor of a denomination that practises "believer's" baptism. He once told me that he would rebaptize anyone who had been baptized as a baby and who wanted to join his church. We were good friends so we could speak frankly without offending each other. He explained that he believed an active faith was part of Baptism. Since, from his perspective, that faith had not been active in the person baptized as a baby, he felt it was important to baptize the person when they actually experienced the faith as their own.

I agreed with him that an active faith is part of

Baptism. Faith is active in the parents and sponsors who bring a baby for baptism. As the child grows, we expect the parents and sponsors to kindle the faith within the child so that each baptized person becomes a mature and faith-filled person. Lutherans believe that such growth is the work of the Holy Spirit.

My friend's emphasis was on the actual experience of the person. If I understand what he was trying to tell me, when the person really believed, then that person should be baptized. That's why Christian groups which share his view don't baptize babies.

There happened to be a fellow in town who had been baptized as a baby and then rebaptized in my friend's church as an adult. Later on, he experienced a fresh awakening of his faith at still another church in town, and they wanted to baptize him for yet a third time. "So," I asked my friend, "didn't he get it right at your church either?"

Growing up in the church

Parents have their children baptized. As they promised at the baptisms, they bring their children to church to worship and to learn. They set a good example for their children. Finally the time comes when the children begin to grow up and to decide things for themselves.

So we take time to make sure that they are thoroughly taught the things about faith that upstanding young Lutherans should know. Lutherans spend a great deal more time on this than most denominations. After two or three years of confirmation classes, usually somewhere around age 14 or 15, the confirmands publicly declare that the faith into which they were baptized is their faith. This practice varies a lot from congregation to congregation.

Sometimes it really happens that way. Unfortunately, the fact is that, in spite of our good intentions, many of the young people who make their confirmation vows seldom return to participate in worship after their confirmation.

Sometimes this happens because parents send their children to Sunday school but never bring them to worship. All too often, instead of seeing confirmation as something they do, they see it as a sort of graduation ceremony. School's out and they are "outa here."

What happens at worship and in the rest of the life of the congregation is strange to them because it hasn't been part of their routine. With everything that is happening to them at that age, it is no wonder they don't want to add church to their agenda.

Some congregations try to counter this by finding people who can really relate to teens and who are willing to help and spend time with the kids. Other congregations delay the age for instruction and confirmation, feeling that a bit more maturity is needed.

One of the problems we face is that for many of us who come from a European background, confirmation is important for reasons that have very little to do with faith. Confirmation has traditionally been a rite of passage, a ceremony where people say that you are no longer a child (something similar to the Jewish Bar Mitzvah).

Such families may have very little to do with any congregation but when that special age arrives, they demand that their children be confirmed. Sadly, most pastors know from experience that they probably won't see these families again until there is a wedding or a funeral.

Sometimes Confirmation opens doors which draw one or more members of the family into a deeper faith. And as a result they **do** get involved in the life of the congregation. That's why I feel we should always be as gracious as we can be in trying to go along with such requests.

Membership

Confirmation doesn't make people members of the church. They became members when they were baptized. If you are baptized in a Lutheran congregation, you are automatically a member of that congregation. Other people must join the congregation by a letter of transfer or through affirmation of faith.

44

The rites and sacraments of the church are not reserved exclusively for members. However, many Lutheran pastors have become reluctant to marry or bury people who are not congregational members, or to baptize their babies.

This example of a couple who once made an appointment with me to discuss their plans to marry may help you to understand why this happens. I had never met them before. When they arrived at my office, they asked to see the church. They took one look and said, "We're sorry. We were looking for something much more impressive so that it would look good in our wedding pictures." At least they were honest.

While churches work to make the community a better place and to offer many social services such as counseling, day care, and food banks, our religious services are meant for the community of faith as places where we grow together as people of God, where our faith is nourished and continues to grow. In the fast-paced world with all its pressures, we need a place where we can help each other along the way.

Congregational membership demands and offers a lot more than an impressive backdrop for wedding pictures. It includes caring about the other people who are part of that congregation, sharing their joys and struggles, helping to pay the bills, teaching the children and visiting the sick, praying and playing and laughing and crying together, and all the other things that families, including this family of God, do together.

Holy Communion

What I am going to say about Holy Communion may be a bit different from what happens in the Lutheran congregation you attend. At the National Convention of the ELCIC held in Edmonton in 1991, the ELCIC adopted a *Statement on Sacramental Practices*. It explains our theology and how we put that into practice as it applies to Baptism and Communion.

There was very little disagreement about Baptism, but what the Statement said about Communion was different from what a significant number of Lutherans were used to. When the Convention overwhelmingly approved the Statement, it also passed a resolution that said that the Statement is "a guideline for congregations and is not binding on them."

In principle, every baptized person who wants to receive Communion in an ELCIC congregation should be able to receive Communion. This is called "communion of the baptized."

Traditionally, many Lutherans were not willing to welcome non-Lutherans to commune with them. In fact, they often would not even include Lutherans from another congregation. This practice is known as closed or close Communion and is still adhered to in most congregations in the Lutheran Church—Canada, another Lutheran group which I talk about in "All in the family."

It is also the practice of a number of other denominations. So it is wise to ask if it is all right for you to receive Communion when visiting a different congregation lest you cause offense for your host and embarrassment for yourself.

As a pastor I have always felt that Communion is the Lord's Supper, not the Lutheran's supper. Many ELCIC pastors had always invited every baptized Christian to commune with us. In 1991 the ELCIC officially agreed with us.

What about the children?

Now here comes the wrinkle. It began to occur to people that if we said that every baptized Christian was welcome to commune, what about the children? After all, they're baptized too.

For many years, the normal time for people to receive Communion for the first time was on the day of their Confirmation, or on the following Sunday. Some congregations made a big production out of this by having a public examination on the Sunday before Confirmation, Confirmation Sunday the following week, and finally, First Communion on the third Sunday. This is still the custom in some of our congregations.

However, in the 1960s, many denominations, including Lutherans, began to question why First Communion should follow Confirmation. First Communion gradually started to move to a time around age ten when children and parents would attend classes about Holy Communion. After that, if the child, the parents, and the pastor agreed that the child was "ready," the child began to receive Communion.

This practice met strong resistance from some people who objected that traditional Lutheran teaching regarding proper preparation was not being taken seriously enough. Although the new practice is still not accepted in a number of our congregations, I suspect it will eventually become the norm.

At the same time, there were other people who questioned **any** age limit and openly challenged what it meant to be "ready." "If God's grace is a free gift," they asked, "what does it mean to be properly prepared to receive that gift?"

Suddenly Lutherans were faced with the question of giving Communion to babies. The idea made many people nervous. It challenged some basic assumptions.

At the Convention in Edmonton, the ELCIC said that babies could commune. This was a historic move that is now forcing similar debates throughout the Lutheran world and throughout the entire Christian world.

The debate has not ended in the ELCIC. It continues from congregation to congregation. In actual numbers, very few babies receive Communion, but the practice has been established and is growing.

How do you commune a baby? Some break off a tiny piece of communion wafer or bread and dip it into the wine and place it in the baby's mouth. Others give the baby a tiny piece of bread. Still others touch the baby's tongue with a drop or two of wine on a spoon. Common sense and some sensitivity seem to be the key.

Personally, I've been delighted to have the children join us at Communion. Now they are not only nourished by the Word. They fully share in the family meal. My hunch is that as these children grow into adults, fewer of them will walk out the door; Sunday worship will be an important part of their lives, a place where they belong and have not been excluded.

Some practical stuff about Communion

I've mentioned that the ELCIC is committed to practising "eucharistic hospitality." That means every baptized Christian is welcome to commune with us.

Maybe I'd better sort out some of the words we use. You will hear Lutherans call Holy Communion by a number of other names. The Lord's Supper is the usual one but more and more Lutherans talk about the Eucharist, a word that means thanksgiving. A few mention the Sacrament of the Altar, and one or two even call it Mass.

Only an ordained minister may preside at Communion. An exception is sometimes made where an ordained minister is not available for a long time. Then the bishop will appoint a layperson for a specific period of time and only for that specific situation. Properly trained laypeople may also help out in the leadership of the service, including the distribution of the bread and wine.

There are really no set patterns for how Communion must be celebrated except that, according to our Lutheran Confessions, we prefer that it be celebrated every Sunday in every congregation. Although once it would have been considered unusual, it is becoming more common to celebrate Communion at weddings and funerals.

These practices are still not what people are used to nor do they take place in every Lutheran congregation. Some congregations have communion services only a few times a year, while others have it monthly, or every other week. But we are moving in the direction of weekly Communion as a normal part of worship.

Lutherans stand, kneel, or sit to receive Communion. In some congregations you move up in one continuous line to the people serving Communion. In other places one group at a time goes to the front of the church and stands while the ministers serve them. In still others, people stand in a circle around the altar and after one person is communed that person then communes the person standing next to them and so on around the circle.

Some congregations use a variety of kinds of bread. Others never use anything except a tiny round wafer that many people claim tastes like styrofoam and which usually sticks to the roof of your mouth until it gets moist.

We normally use wine, although a few congregations offer grape juice. In some congregations everyone drinks from the same cup, while other congregations use little, individual glasses. In some congregations the glasses are prepoured while other congregations fill them from a common pouring cup or chalice.

Some place the bread in your hand, but a few feed you by putting it right in your mouth. Some hand you the cup, while others hold the cup for you. Some people prefer to dip the bread into the wine. (This is called intinction.)

People who commune usually receive both the bread and the wine, but sometimes an exception needs to be made for health or other reasons. Receiving only the bread or the wine is allowed. Common sense and courtesy should make us as gracious about this as the One who is host of this meal.

I used to commune one person who was totally paralyzed and who could not swallow either the bread or the wine. In this case I simply said to her "The body and blood of Christ given and shed for you." The gift of God's grace is what is important, not the mechanics.

Some people cannot come to worship because they are sick or shut-ins. Some congregations train laypeople to take Holy Communion to these persons following the Sunday service. Most pastors also make periodic visits to these people and celebrate the Sacrament with them.

Preparing for Communion

According to Martin Luther, special preparation for Communion can be a helpful discipline, but in the end all you really need is a believing heart.

I remember one occasion very vividly. My parishioner was a very old man who didn't seem to know what was happening around him any more. He lived in a nursing home. He and I were in a room all by ourselves. I had to speak very loudly so that he could hear me. My words echoed back at me in that empty room and I felt a bit foolish. I wasn't sure that he could understand me. I wondered what I was doing there. I began to celebrate the Sacrament with him anyway.

I still wasn't sure that he knew what was going on. Then I began to say the Lord's Prayer. I saw his lips begin to move and a tear trickle down his cheek. He received the bread and the wine with a clear and steady gaze of gratitude. Then he lapsed back into that shadowy world where he had been living.

Even if he had showed no response, I would have trusted in the gifts of grace given in Communion. God alone knows what lies in the depths of our hearts.

Some people like to fast, to go without eating, before they commune. Others like to talk over what has been going on in their lives with God in prayer. Some will go to the pastor for private confession. Occasionally, someone will go to another person with whom they are having a disagreement and try to patch things up before they come to Communion. Still others will take time to read their Bibles and devotional books about the meaning of Communion and to meditate on these things. These are all worthwhile and can help to make your receiving of Communion a rich and rewarding experience.

Learning for a lifetime

I don't think that anyone can possibly understand the full mystery of Holy Communion in one lifetime. You can spend a lifetime learning. Here is a sketch of a few things that I have learned.

To quote the *Statement on Sacramental Practices*, "Holy Communion is a means of grace through which the crucified and risen Christ awakens faith, saves, forgives, unites, gives life, comforts and strengthens God's people for the work to which they are called in the world."

Receiving Communion is a very personal matter. In the statements "The body of Christ given for you. The blood of Christ shed for you," the words "for you" remind us that God's grace touches us personally.

At the same time, this meal is a symbol of the unity of the church. In it you are reminded that you are part of the Body of Christ—a community that extends past the four walls of the place where you are receiving Communion, a community that reaches out to include everyone who ever has or ever will commune.

Holy Communion is a celebration of the goodness of God. It is a little taste of the feast that we will celebrate in heaven. It stirs up memories of what Jesus has done for us.

See what I mean? Pondering the depth of those mysteries can easily fill a lifetime.

Here comes the groom

You may be reading this book because you asked a Lutheran pastor to marry you and that pastor suggested that you find out more about the ELCIC first.

Some Lutheran pastors won't talk to you about a wedding unless you are a member. Others see it as a chance to help the couple think about what it means to be a Christian.

If you just want to get married and you don't care who does it, I suggest you try City Hall. More and more communities provide wedding chapels where someone will marry you. For those who like a bit more pomp and circumstance, an increasing number of commercial companies in the wedding business will cater to your every whim. They will take care of every detail and provide you with a wonderful ceremony and all the sentimental things your heart desires.

Hopefully, you don't just want the pastor to marry you because he or she conducts an impressive ceremony, or because this church was the place where your parents were married, or because the building is so photogenic.

A church wedding should be thought of as a marriage that takes place **in a congregation** rather than in that congregation's building. This is a chance for the people of God to gather to witness the union of a couple before God, to pray for that couple, to ask for God's blessing on this marriage, and to celebrate the goodness of God that is shared in such joyous occasions. All that other stuff is really incidental.

Marriage preparation

More and more Lutheran congregations insist that couples take time to prepare for marriage, even if they have already been living together for some time. This is also true for couples who may have been married before. If a previous marriage ended in divorce, we try to make sure that the couple has a chance to learn something that may help them avoid making the same mistakes again.

Sometimes the minister conducts special classes or has a series of conversations with just the couple. At other times, couples who are planning to marry come from several congregations to attend special classes. A variety of leaders speak on different subjects such as financial planning, relationships, communication, sexuality, and so on.

A number of ministers provide couples with a questionnaire that helps them to compare their values and their attitudes about a variety of things that they are likely to face in their lives. Then the couple and the pastor take time to talk these things over.

Sometimes couples discover that they already knew each other very well. Once in a while they find that they have nothing in common except sexual attraction.

After I sorted through a set of these questions with one couple, it was obvious that they really didn't know each other very well and that they needed to do a lot of talking with each other. They had been living together for a while and had decided that they should get married. A few days after our visit they called and said that the wedding was off. They had decided to go their separate ways. They were very grateful that they had discovered how little they really had in common before they headed into what they both agreed would have been a disastrous marriage.

Marriage preparation can also be a time when a couple can talk about religious questions and issues. Sometimes the questions can be very simple.

One couple asked me if I would teach them how to pray. No one had ever helped them to understand that prayer is simply a matter of talking things over with God in an ordinary conversation, like the one that you would have with any good and trusted friend. That opened a new world for both of them.

I learned that nothing should be taken for granted in marriage preparation. I always used to include a little talk about the facts of life, even though I suspected that some of the couples knew more about it than I did. I also found out that we often pretend to know more about sex than we do because we are supposed to be sexually sophisticated in this society.

One nurse thanked me for the information. "Everyone always thinks that nurses know all this stuff," she said. "So I never had the chance to find out any of it."

Marriage is hard work. I can not predict whether a couple will have a successful marriage or not. I have seen marriages I was sure were made in heaven end in divorce. I have also seen people who I wasn't sure should ever be married to each other struggle through some tough times together and develop a strong and loving relationship.

Many communities offer two programs designed to make marriages stronger and more loving. They are called *Marriage Encounter* and *Marriage Enrichment*. Both these courses are for couples who are already married. *Engaged Encounter* is available for couples who are planning to marry.

Diane and I helped to found *Lutheran Marriage Encounter* in Ontario. It was a helpful experience for us. We would recommend it to couples with good marriages who want to make them even better.

The arrangements

I used to tell couples planning their weddings that there were three people who had to agree on the details—the two of them, and me. "I don't care what your mom or your cousin Mildred think," I would say. "It's your wedding, and you are going to be left with the memories of it."

There is a lot of flexibility in a Lutheran wedding ceremony. Most Lutheran pastors will work with you to make your wedding fit your personal choices—if you approach them properly. However, some busy pastors insist on limiting your choices because they know from experience what will and will not work in their setting and in their timetable. It may all be new to you, but it's soon very old hat to most ministers.

As a member of the clergy, I owe it to other clergy to pass something on to you. Nothing tempts a minister to use words no Christian should utter, or to contemplate murderous acts quicker, than a couple who make all their arrangements before making a simple telephone call to ask if they can be married by that minister at the time they had in mind.

Ministers have very full appointment books. A wedding usually means many hours of preparation, not to mention the time for the ceremony. On one weekend in a small parish I had three weddings scheduled. To make matters worse, someone in the parish died that same weekend. Occasionally, my weekends were booked more than a year in advance for a wedding.

I have a standard announcement that I make at weddings: "Please don't take pictures during the ceremony. We'll pose for you at the end to give you time to take whatever pictures you want. If you brought confetti in your pocket or purse, please take it home with you the same way." I found that solves many problems.

A recent phenomenon is the video camera. A bit of common sense and cooperation, with some planning, can help a couple preserve their wedding on video without the camera getting in the way of the ceremony.

More and more congregations set fees for an organist, the caretaker, the use of the building and for the minister's time. It usually doesn't cover the real costs, especially when people often spend more on the flowers, but it does help.

I know one minister who tried to get out of having weddings for people who didn't attend his church by charging a higher and higher fee. It didn't work out the way he expected. People figured that if he charged so much, he must be one of the best. More people than ever started showing up on his doorstep asking if he would marry them.

Who can and who can't

There are no particular rules in the ELCIC about which couples pastors may marry and which couples they may not marry. It's usually left with the pastor to decide.

No one approves of divorce. Although the Bible says that Jesus recognized adultery as the only grounds for divorce, many of us take the position that some marriages are better ended to stop a lot of pain and misery. We also feel that divorced people should have the chance to try again.

I would not marry a couple just because of pregnancy. I believe that starting a marriage because of a mistake is a poor way to begin. But I have married several young couples who were very much in love and who forgot to wait for their wedding day to start their family.

Variations and gimmicks

Diane and I wrote our own wedding service. It was the thing to do at the time. I have married people in homes and in backyards. I once even married a couple at their annual barbecue with about 100 of their friends standing around on the lawn. There have been guitars and flutes and harps and trumpets and even bagpipes played at weddings I've conducted.

I've heard *The Wedding Song* and *Bridge over Troubled Waters* sung at many weddings. I've never made a fuss over the music if the people doing it were good at

55

singing or playing, and the words were in keeping with a Christian view of marriage. I have even helped a couple rewrite an offending line just so they could use a song they found meaningful. But I have drawn the line at *Good-bye Mama* and *Help Me Make It through the Night.*

Some congregations have well-trained organists or directors of music. They can also give you valuable advice which will allow your music to do all that you hoped it would and still be suitable for a church service.

People tell me that I'm quite a bit more flexible than your average Lutheran minister. Apparently most Lutheran ministers won't put up with much nonsense when it comes to weddings. At the moment, we seem to be in more conservative times and fads are fading away.

A word of advice from a pastor who has married many couples. Over the years I've found that the simple ceremonies are usually the most impressive and memorable for all the right reasons.

Funerals

It might surprise you to know that the part of being a parish pastor that I liked best was funerals. I don't mean that I enjoyed funerals. But I found it was often a time when people were the most real with me. In most cases, funerals turned out to be an opportunity when we could talk about the things in life that really matter.

When I was in the parish, I seldom refused to take anyone's funeral, unless the person was not a member and I just couldn't fit anything else into my schedule. This is becoming a bigger problem for pastors than people realize.

In some of our larger cities, there are many people who call themselves Lutherans, and a lot who don't call themselves anything but "Christian" in nodding recognition of the fact that they were once baptized somewhere. These people are growing old and dying. Suddenly it becomes very urgent that a Lutheran pastor be called, or in some cases any pastor at all.

It is not unusual for some pastors to have four or five funerals in a week. Add this to all the other work a pastor still has to do and you begin to realize why some pastors simply can't meet the demand and refuse to bury anyone who is not part of their parish.

At the time of a death, the pastor can give you comfort and advice and can help you prepare for the funeral.

If the family wanted me to, I would go with them to the funeral home as they made arrangements with the funeral director. I found that most funeral directors were very caring and thoroughly honest. But there are a few that will take advantage of a family's grief. Just having the minister present, even if he or she never says a word, usually keeps a director with a touch of larceny in line.

Normally, there is no eulogy in a Lutheran funeral service. Whenever I could I would gather family and friends together to talk with me about the person who had died. I used their comments to plan the points I needed to make in my funeral sermon.

Of course the pastor conducts the funeral, but people often are not aware of how a pastor can help afterward. Most of our clergy are specially trained to help people who are grieving. Grief work takes a long time and can mean many visits over many months, in some cases even years. While many people do not turn to a pastor for help with their grief, a significant number do. Sometimes pastors will form a support group by putting bereaved people in touch with each other.

Making plans

While I have you thinking about funerals, think about a few things you can and should do. The first one is to make your will. Don't just say that you'll get around to it sometime. Do it. (After I said that enough times to enough people, Diane dragged me off to a lawyer to see that I had my own will drawn up.)

You should also consider the form on your driver's license that allows your body to be used for medical purposes if you meet with an accidental death. Many other lives can be saved by taking time to fill in that form, if you feel that such a gesture is appropriate.

There are no religious reasons why you shouldn't and some that suggest why you should. If you do decide to sign the form, discuss your decision with the rest of your family so that they understand your wishes in this matter.

Something else that you can do that will greatly help your family is to write down the things that you would like to have happen at your funeral. You may even want to sit down with a reputable funeral director and preplan the funeral arrangements. This is not morbid or sick, and many families have appreciated the thoughtfulness.

While you're at it, why not take time to talk about what you would want to have happen if you should become terminally ill and were only being kept alive by machines. This is a very difficult and painful decision that becomes even harder if the person on the machines is in a coma, and the family is left guessing about that person's wishes.

Personally, I think that the loving and proper thing to do is to pull the plug. That is what I would want my family and friends to do for me. I don't see this as playing God. I think it is leaving the life of a loved one for whom you have done all that is humanly possible in the hands of a loving God.

Death is the one thing in your life that you can be absolutely certain of. So why not face it? Facing death can be a big help in learning to face life.

The service

I think that I will always remember Ed Schlitt's funeral. Ed was one of those faithful Christians every congregation cherishes. He was 83 at the time of his death. He had been a founder of the congregation where his funeral was held.

We gathered together at the church for Ed's funeral—family, friends, and members of the congregation, some who barely knew him. Ed's coffin sat at the front of the church where he had so faithfully worshiped and served year after year.

We sang some of the hymns he loved, and remembered him. I talked about the faith that had sustained him, the faith that could sustain everyone present.

We celebrated Holy Communion at Ed's funeral. People commented that it was one of the most joyous services they had ever attended. Most of us had tears in our eyes at one time or another, but they were not bitter tears. They were happy tears and healing tears.

In the middle of a large city, this funeral helped the members of that congregation, as well as Ed's family and friends, experience what it means to be part of the family of God. That's what every funeral service should do.

The casket is closed at a funeral service, and it may be covered with a pall. As testimony to the presence of the living Christ, a paschal candle is lit and stands by the casket if the funeral takes place in a church and the congregation uses such a candle.

Viewing the body before a funeral, however, can be a helpful part of grieving for people, especially when they have not been present at the death. It can help them come to grips with the reality of this death.

For the same reason, some pastors also ask that the casket be lowered into the grave while the family watches. Some Lutherans, particularly if they come from Latin America, also want to help fill in the grave rather than leave that task to strangers.

Some families prefer to have a small funeral followed by the committal service attended by immediate family and a few close friends. Then, at a time when it is easier for others to attend, a memorial service is held at the church.

Many families choose cremation. Diane and I have indicated that this is what we would both prefer for ourselves. In such cases, committal is done as part of the funeral service or it may be done at the crematorium.

Funerals are not for the dead but for the living. They are a time for grieving, for remembering, and for saying good-bye, for tears and sometimes also for great joy. Sometimes they are the beginning of healing if the death was particularly tragic or if there were quarrels that were never mended, hatreds that were never forgiven.

Funerals can be a time for discovering the strength and hope that Christianity offers. When our son Jed died, I experienced two different emotions. I was very, very angry with God. I was also very, very grateful that I believed in a God who loved me enough to take all my anger, accept it, and still love me.

Celebrating the pilgrimage

I understand why people want the church to be part of their hatching, matching, and dispatching. These are important times in their journey through life, times that should be celebrated as the sacred moments that they are. The real tragedy is when people no longer care if the church is involved.

How sad it would be if no one celebrated when we were born, or noticed that we were growing into an adult, or rejoiced at our wedding, or cared enough to comment on our dying.

The rites and sacraments of the church are there to help us remember that God celebrates and notices and rejoices and cares. They are there to get us going on our journey with God and to sustain and nourish our faith along the way. And finally, the church is there to commit us for time and eternity into the hands of our loving God.

Chapter 4

Photo: Kenn Ward

What happens the rest of the week

Even in the smallest congregations, Sunday morning worship is usually only the start of a very busy week of activities. For those who get involved, some of the best things in their lives happen through their congregation.

I'm not going to try to describe everything that goes on in our Lutheran churches. The activities in congregations vary with the size, location and interest of those who gather there. Some church buildings buzz with activity almost every minute of the week. Others are seldom opened except for Sunday worship.

Evangelical Lutheran Women

A good place to start is Evangelical Lutheran Women (ELW). In most of our congregations, you will find a busy member-group of the ELCIC's only official auxiliary organization.

The size and composition of the group depend on the congregation. Some concentrate on Bible study and meet regularly for some lively discussions. Others are heavily into community service and social-action projects.

A number of ELW groups also make sure that the social functions at the church run smoothly by catering for meals and serving coffee and tea at receptions. While many ELW groups take pride in this form of service, an increasing number of them do not want to be stereotyped into this role. More and more we have begun to see the men helping in the kitchens of our congregations as well.

For some Lutheran women, life in a congregation without ELW would be unthinkable. Others would never consider attending an ELW meeting.

Unfortunately, some people have an image of ELW that is really only a caricature, an image of a bunch of old ladies who attend boring meetings, who sit around sipping tea and gossiping, or who do nothing but act as a sort of catering service for the congregation. As with all stereotypes, there is a little bit of truth in the description some of the time, but even where the ELW is made up of more elderly women, this caricature is very superficial and unfair.

ELW groups have produced bonds between women that have helped them to see each other through death and disaster. One woman who had moved to Toronto from a foreign country once told me that, if it hadn't been for the friendship and support of the women in her ELW group, she doubts that she would have been able to make it through the first years of settling into the new life that had been forced upon her.

ELW provides an opportunity for women to gather to study God's Word, to develop leadership skills, to share talents and creativity, and to express their faith through action. Even people who are not members often find that it is worth sharing in ELW ideas through the pages of ELW's magazine *Esprit*.

You will also find women's organizations that are not part of the official auxiliary in a number of our congregations. Some of these groups, such as Ladies Aid, have a long history that comes from one of the church bodies that came before the ELCIC. Others have simply developed out of local circumstances.

The men

There is no official organization for men in the ELCIC. Perhaps our men don't feel a need for it.

However, in some congregations, men get together for a prayer breakfast once a month. There may be a special speaker, but there is no heavy agenda. Good coffee and conversation are priorities.

After the Montreal massacre, our chaplain at the University of Toronto, Bob Shantz, organized a men's group on campus to give men an opportunity to explore what it means to be a man in our society.

Both efforts have been appreciated and may be symptoms of things yet to come. Men haven't had much practice talking with each other about faith and feelings. Perhaps the time is coming when they will feel free enough to try.

Youth

Every two years, one ELCIC event happens which attracts more ELCIC people than any other. This is the Canadian Lutheran Youth Gathering (CLYG). Lutheran teens travel from every part of the country to meet for several exciting days. For some, it is a time that will forever change their lives.

A CLYG is filled with workshops and worship, inspirational speakers and musicians, lots of cheers and laughter, and sometimes a few tears as a teen finally finds someone who will listen and understand. For at least those few days, a few of our kids discover how great it can really be to be part of the church that calls itself Lutheran.

CLYGs are only one opportunity for youth to get involved in our church. Many of our youth never attend a CLYG and still find church rewarding. Youth need encouragement. When a person or a congregation really cares about kids and provides many activities for them to be involved in, the rewards are tremendous. It is no coincidence that such congregations are among our most vibrant and dynamic.

Non-church groups

Some congregations make their building available to community groups as part of their ministry of outreach. Sometimes a congregation will organize a group because there is a need in the community. People from the community may be an active part of this group and yet never attend worship on Sunday morning.

Alcoholics Anonymous and many other self-help groups find homes in Lutheran buildings. A counseling service, often jointly operated by several congregations in the community, may have some office space in one of our buildings.

Beavers, Cubs, Scouts, Venturers, Brownies and Guides are often sponsored by the congregation. Occasionally, a proud pastor gets to present a Religion-in-Life badge to a member of Boy Scouts or Girl Guides who has done special service in the life of the congregation.

Nursery schools and daycare centers also use some of the church's space. Sometimes these are run by a group of people from the congregation. In other cases, they are private businesses which simply lease the space.

Sunday school

It may be my imagination, but I think I see signs that more and more parents are starting to bring their children to Sunday school again. Attendance dropped off for a few years, but a younger generation of parents seems to be rethinking what their children are learning about right and wrong, and about what life is really all about.

Some adults are also discovering that Sunday school is not just for kids. A growing number of congregations have adult classes with a whole range of interesting subjects. Such classes are still more the exception than the rule, but writers, publishers, and pastors keep trying. In most congregations, you don't have to be a member to attend classes. You don't even have to be baptized. Sometimes there is a small fee to help to pay for materials, but more often than not they are free.

Sunday school doesn't always happen on Sundays. Some congregations fit a time for classes into another part of the week, sometimes combining instruction with recreation and a meal.

The Lutheran church takes great pride in the quality of its educational resources. The folks at Wood Lake Books are justifiably proud of *The Whole People of God* curriculum which is used in most United and Anglican church congregations as well as in a number of Presbyterian and Lutheran churches.

However, even in a book published by Wood Lake Books, I have to tell you that we Lutherans also publish some great stuff through Augsburg Fortress Publishing House which has its own stores in Kitchener, Ontario, and Calgary, Alberta. End of commercial.

Even the best materials can't do their job unless they are used by good teachers. Fortunately there are many willing people around who care about our kids and what they are learning.

Still the best curriculum with the best teachers has little lasting impact on children if it is not backed up by solid parental example. Sunday school is not a baby-sitting service for parents who want a break for a couple of hours.

By the way, if you really get involved in the learning end of our church, you will soon discover that the people who learn the most are the teachers. These days most material is set up for the person who has a lot of enthusiasm but may not have much teaching experience or the time to do a lot of preplanning.

The choir

This is my favorite group in the congregation. Now that I'm not up at the front leading the service, on most Sundays you'll find me sitting at the back in the choir, happily booming away in the bass section. Most of the time I even manage to sing the right notes in the right key.

I think that choirs are best heard and not seen. A good choir can help to add a richer dimension to the worship of any congregation. Basically we are worship leaders and helpers rather than performers, although deep down most of us are hams at heart.

What you hear on Sunday morning is a very small part of life in a choir. There are hours and hours of practice and learning, as well as an awful lot of good fun and fellowship.

Choirs come in all sizes, shapes and sounds. Some have the help of professional musicians. Others are just a few good friends who get together to sing a song for a special occasion so that the service that day will seem extra special. Many of us have more enthusiasm than musical ability, but we are out to give God glory rather than win the approval of the local music critic.

Other groups

Groups come and go in congregations for a variety of reasons. There are young adults, couples, singles, people interested in ecology, people seeking richer marriages, those who want to help a refugee family, the recently bereaved, film clubs, discussion groups—whatever happens to interest a group of people in the church who find it worthwhile to get together to share a common interest.

When I was in college, our congregation put on a Sunday dinner once a month for college students. It wasn't a very big thing, but for some lonely college kids it was a place to meet other Lutherans and to share a meal and a few laughs. At least one marriage and several lasting friendships came out of those Sunday meals.

That's really the point of all this activity. Each activity is a chance for the people of God to get to know each other better, to learn to be the Church together.

The Bible says that we are God's children, brothers and sisters in Christ, family. In healthy families, each family member is loved, cherished and supported in good times and in bad.

More and more congregations are reaching out to others, welcoming them into the family through one group or another that meets a certain need that person has.

I won't pretend that this happens in every congregation, or that every person is warmly welcomed. Some congregations act more like a dysfunctional family than the kind of family God wants us to become. But never underestimate the power of the Holy Spirit. A real person with a real need has brought new life and purpose to more than one congregation.

Oh those meals!

Lutherans love to find excuses to get together for a meal. I think most congregations in other denominations are like that too. Every congregation has to have at least one or two good feeds a year.

My favorite meals are those potluck suppers. Everyone brings something. There are usually enough different dishes so that there is plenty for both the main course and dessert. Often there is usually way too much, but nobody minds.

Casseroles are the main ingredient for a good potluck meal. As we welcome more and more newcomers into our midst, the meals are becoming more and more exotic. Sitting next to the Swedish meatballs and the German sauerkraut, you might find Oriental pepper steak, Mexican tortillas, West African groundnut stew, and Indian samosas.

Whatever language was used to translate the recipes into the various dishes assembled for this meal, the food says that people gathered for this feast understand hospitality and sharing. It is an extension of the meal of Holy Communion which, if you will recall, began as part of a meal.

A lesser meal (lesser in the quantity of food, but not lesser in the amount of fellowship) is coffee hour. More than a few people have claimed that Lutherans should proclaim coffee time as our third sacrament. More good is often done during a friendly chat over a cup of coffee or tea than we could ever imagine.

Camping and retreats

A number of church camps are scattered across Canada. To work at improving their operations and programing, most belong to LOMIC (Lutheran Outdoor Ministries in Canada). While many of the camps concentrate on children's programs, several also offer camping opportunities for adults and families.

Church camp provided the first chance I had to begin to learn that there was more to being a Christian than what I had seen in my family and in our congregation. One of my special childhood memories is of a flotilla of crosses lit with candles drifting down the stream at Camp Edgewood on the final night of camp.

A growing number of congregations regularly sponsor retreats. Retreats sometimes take place at camps, but there are a wide variety of places available for such events. One of my favorite retreat settings is a canoe trip.

Usually a retreat provides an opportunity for a group of people to get away for a day or two to worship and learn, to take time to get a little closer to God and to each other. Retreats can be as solemn or as silly, as structured or informal, as the group feels they need to be.

I have found that a retreat is a good way to give a group the chance to do some serious long-range planning. It can also be a very good way to get away from everyday pressures and to relax. Both types of retreat can be equally rewarding.

Bazaars and fundraising

The ELCIC hasn't quite figured out whether to like or to loathe bazaars. The problem is that, when we became a new denomination in 1986, we brought together two different traditions.

One of our founding groups felt that bazaars and the like had no place in the church. They felt that people might get the false impression that they were somehow winning favor with God by buying something from the church. They believed that the church should be able to raise money through the charity of its own members and not ask other people to support it.

The other founding group saw bazaars as a good excuse to get people working together, in the belief that such experiences build a stronger sense of community. They are usually a lot of fun, and the bit of money that they earn is a bonus.

Bazaars also helped Lutherans build bridges with people of other denominations in the community, people who might never visit each other in their churches without the round of church bazaars and suppers. When I served in Listowel, Ontario, the Lutheran church was famous for its sauerkraut suppers which old-timers from many denominations in the town fondly recalled.

Whether bazaars come or go, Lutherans will always find ways to work together and to have a good time doing it.

Community

A healthy and alive congregation is formed by a community of believers who are actively learning, serving, sharing the gospel, and providing needed support in a whole variety of ways.

The worship of that congregation grows out of the things the people of that Christian community share with each other. Worship also challenges the members of the congregation to greater possibilities of community as they live and love and learn and laugh and cry and celebrate together. Church is not just a one-hour-on-Sunday-morning experience, but adds something worthwhile to all the other hours and days of the week too.

As a little girl once so wisely said, "Church is that place with a plus on top."

Chapter 5

Photo: Neil Thomsen

What we believe

Some people claim that it doesn't matter what you believe, just as long as you believe something. Wrong. What we believe matters very much. In fact it's really a matter of life and death.

Mother Teresa, for example, has some very strong beliefs. Do you think that it doesn't matter what she believes? How about what Hitler believed? Or Gandhi? Or Martin Luther?

Some people claim that all religions are really like a group of buses heading down the same highway. It doesn't matter which bus you board because all the passengers are eventually going to reach the same destination.

Did you ever watch buses leave a bus station? They

don't all head down the same highway. No matter what direction they start heading, it's not very long before they are traveling to all sorts of different places. There's no way I would hop on the first bus that pulled up to the station without finding out where it was headed. Otherwise I would never be sure where I would end up.

I think some of the people who use bus talk really mean all those different Christian denominations when they are talking about religions. Fair enough. It does seem to make sense that people who belong to the Christian family should all expect to end up at home with God eventually, no matter what denominational label they happen to wear.

As for me, I prefer to ride the Lutheran bus.

God-talk

I'm going to take you for a quick tour along the route that our Lutheran bus travels. The more traditional way of talking about this is doing theology. Doing theology means to study God and deals with our questions about God.

I know that there are theologians who have given birth to theological ideas and lectures that only a mother could love. I'm going to try to do theology that uses Lutheran ideas but doesn't bog you down in all the scholarly stuff.

Every one of us is a theologian of sorts because we all have questions about God. Whenever we begin to wonder about why we were born, or why bad things happen to good people, or what God is really like, we are doing theology.

Each one of us has our own basic set of beliefs about life. Scratch around under the surface a bit and you will discover what those beliefs say about God and you.

For instance, a person who believes that you have to do to others before they do to you has accepted a way of believing that is very different from what Jesus taught. On the other hand, a person who believes that God helps those who help themselves operates from a belief that God may have created the world, but we are given some responsibility for what happens to God's creation.

I think you get the picture. As I talk about what we Lutherans believe, I hope that you begin to think about what you believe too.

Jesus

To understand God, you have to start with Jesus. We believe that this Jew, who was born in Bethlehem, who grew up in Nazareth, lived and taught in ancient Palestine, and who was then crucified in Jerusalem at about 33 years of age, was and is God.

That's where our faith begins and ends. It is that simple and that complicated. At the heart of our faith is not what Jesus taught, but who Jesus is.

Martin Luther developed a slogan that we Lutherans believe is the heart of Christianity: "justification by grace through faith."

What that means is that the way our lives turn out for here and eternity has nothing to do with how much we try to be good and do good, or how badly we screw up trying. Salvation is a pure act of grace on God's part.

God's love for us was shown once and for all in the dying and rising to new life of Jesus Christ. God died on that cross for us. That's God's grace in action.

All God asks us to do is to have faith. Faith is simply another way of saying, "Trust God." God is in charge of our lives. God accepts us. You can bet your life that God, who in Jesus laid his life on the line for you, intends a good and joyous here and now and hereafter for you.

Salvation

Let me try to explain it another way because this idea is so central to Lutheran theology. You have to get this if you really want to understand what makes us tick.

The root meaning of salvation is health or wholeness. When you are completely healthy and whole in body, mind, soul and spirit, and in your relationships with God and humanity, that's salvation.

Salvation is not something that we earn. It is a gift

given to us through Jesus Christ.

Forget the balance sheet idea with St. Peter sitting at the golden gates with a big book where all our deeds are recorded. You know the scenario. The person who has just died appears in front of St. Peter a bit bewildered about the whole business. Peter checks the tally, handing out harps and halos to the good and sadly but sternly turning away those who don't have enough good deeds recorded.

That makes for interesting movies and some great cartoons, but God doesn't work that way. Heaven is not corporate headquarters. It's home.

You can check out how Jesus talks about heaven in the gospel of John, chapter 14. He talks about getting places ready in his Father's house. We are family—God's family—adopted into the family because of Jesus.

God

With Lutherans making such a big deal about Jesus, you might begin to wonder what happens to God in all this. Lutherans are sometimes accused of getting so excited about Jesus that they forget about God, but our beliefs don't really work that way.

There is nothing particularly Lutheran about what we believe about God. Everything we teach is found in the Bible. We insist on that. If you want to talk about God, and you can't find anything in the Bible to back up your opinion, then we won't accept your opinion, because that's all it is—your opinion.

If you can't convince us on the basis of the Bible, we won't accept your opinion even if you stick the most impressive title in front of your name and have a whole denomination backing you up.

Even so, our basic beliefs about who God is are not any different from what the majority of other Christians believe about God. We all talk about God in what is called Trinitarian language. The Trinity—God the Father, God the Son, and God the Holy Spirit—sums up what we know about God.

This Trinitarian language was developed by the early

Christians. They talked about God as the Trinity. You won't find the word "Trinity" in your Bible, but the idea is solidly based on what the Bible teaches about God.

In the Trinity, we know or experience God in three persons. This isn't like having three different gods. We believe that there is only one God.

The problem is trying to explain God who really cannot be explained with human terms. Theologians do all sorts of fancy tricks to try to explain exactly what the Trinity is. In the end they finally say that it is a mystery.

I use Trinitarian language about God because it is faithful to the Bible. Even though it sometimes causes us to get our tongues tangled when we try to talk about God, I haven't found anything that works better. Besides, it helps to keep us humble. And when we're talking about God, that seems to me like a good idea.

The Apostles' Creed

Early Christians had trouble sorting out ideas about the Trinity too. After much talk, they came up with statements that summed up what they believed about God. We call these statements "creeds." The early Christians agreed that these creeds said some things that we know for sure about God.

We Lutherans accept three creeds: the Apostles' Creed, the Nicene Creed, and the Athanasian Creed.

Martin Luther explains the Apostles' Creed with some very good answers in his *Small Catechism*. The Apostles didn't write this creed. However, the people who did believed that they were saying what the Apostles would have said if they had still been around to write it. I'll give you a brief outline here.

The first part of the Creed, or what is called the First Article, talks about God the Father. Most people believe that there is a God. Yet saying that there is a God doesn't really tell us anything about God. Even the Devil believes in God, but the Devil believes that God is the enemy.

We believe in God as Father. I won't get into the problems that this masculine word is causing for some

74

people these days. Historically, "Father" has been meant to describe God as a good and loving parent and was not intended to say that God is male rather than female, because God is not human. God is God. God takes a personal interest in the world, just as loving parents care for their offspring.

We also believe in God the Son, the subject of the Second Article. I've already explained most of this, except to add that we believe that Jesus rules the world (that's that part about sitting at the right hand of the Father) and will come again to judge every person, living and dead.

The Third Article talks about God the Holy Spirit. Even our faith is a gift of God. Faith is the work of the Holy Spirit who builds the Christian Church. This Church has nothing to do with being a Lutheran or any of the other labels we Christians use.

The real Church exists in the hearts of believers and is known only to God. Day after day, the Holy Spirit feeds our faith and makes us strong with God's grace. The Spirit will do that until the day when we enter eternity with our gracious God.

Confessions

If you really want to get into what Lutherans believe in depth, you have to turn to the Lutheran Confessions. Forget the way you usually use that word confession. When you're speaking Lutheran at times like this, you mean an explanation of what we believe, a set of documents that spell out some of the details of our faith. These confessions are found in *The Book of Concord*.

The standard English translation (it was originally written in German and Latin), which was published by Fortress Press in 1959, is 717 pages long. Most Lutherans leave it to their pastor to read and trust that what they hear being taught and preached is laid on this foundation.

The Confessions were written in the 16th century to explain and to defend what Lutherans believe. They were intended to help people discuss their faith. They are still important statements about what we believe.

However, some Lutherans have used them, not to say "We believe this," but to say, "You **must** believe this." Instead of being used as a tool to help Christians talk about their faith, the Confessions have sometimes been used as a weapon to force a certain way of thinking on people.

This is an abuse of the Confessions. You cannot force people to have faith. Faith grows when people can talk things over, study the Bible together, and discover for themselves that these Confessions have important things to teach them about God. Theology is something that we do together rather than something we have done to us by others.

We are convinced that the people who wrote the Confessions had a keen insight into the Christian faith. So we check out what they had to say as we think about what the Bible teaches.

It is a bit like using the river pilots on the St. Lawrence Seaway to get through the tricky parts. Ships' captains could navigate those waters without the pilots. They don't take those risks because the pilots have already mapped out the trouble spots and can help them to travel the route safely.

Unlike the seaway captains, we have to head into uncharted waters some of the time. However the Confessions give us some basic navigating principles to help us avoid getting hung up in shallow and dangerous waters.

The Small Catechism

The one part of The Book of Concord that should be in every Lutheran's library is The Small Catechism. I am amazed at how much good stuff Luther packed into that little book. I've taught many people what Luther had to say and I'm still discovering fresh ideas in his words that I never noticed before.

This little book of questions and answers talks about the basic things every Christian should know. It discusses such things as the Ten Commandments, the

Apostles' Creed, the Lord's Prayer, the Sacraments of Holy Baptism and Holy Communion, and Confession and Absolution.

In Luther's time it was even printed in poster form and hung on the walls of people's homes. Many of the things I've written in this book are based on the Catechism. Sometimes I put them down deliberately. At other times they just come naturally because that little book has been so deeply embedded in my way of thinking.

Worship as theology

Something else that has deeply planted Lutheran theology in me is our worship life. That liturgy and those hymns say what we think about God and our lives with God. Every hymn and phrase in our official books has been carefully selected and debated. A word that didn't say it just right has sometimes been cause for a popular hymn to be left out of the book, or for a congregation to avoid using it even if it did manage to get in there.

If you want to know what the people in a congregation believe, watch what hymns they like and use. Singing those hymns is a way of saying what you believe, reinforcing it, teaching it and learning it. That's why Martin Luther wrote hymns and encouraged us to be a singing church.

Saint and sinner

Have you ever come across a situation where someone has done something really, really terrible and someone else has asked, "How could he (or she) have done something so wicked?" I'm always a bit puzzled by that kind of question. When I take a very hard look at myself in the mirror, I know that, except by the grace of God, I could be just as capable of doing that wicked deed, and that there are times when I do some pretty rotten stuff that amazes me.

Did you ever notice how you might have the best of intentions and promise yourself that you aren't going to do a certain thing? Then you go out and do the very thing that you were so determined that you weren't going to do!

Or you really mess up? You've been having a bad day and you snap at someone. Or you get mad and say things that you regret later. Why do we do that?

Because we are sinners. Paul had the same experience. He talks about it in Romans 7 and says that God's grace in Jesus is stronger than what he calls our slavery to sin. Jesus' death on the cross sets us free to be saints.

This all gets very abstract unless you begin to think about what goes on in our lives. Some folks like to divide life up into things that "good" Christians should and should not do. They may mention a little bit of what they should do. But they usually talk a whole lot about what they should not do—like dancing or listening to certain kinds of music or playing cards or whatever.

According to them, there are things that you can do that make you religious and things that just aren't religious. Some of them really lay down the law about this and are quick to condemn anyone who doesn't play by their rules as not being a real Christian.

Lutherans don't dance to that tune. But we do dance. Some of us take a drink, and we play cards and go to movies, and we do a whole lot of things that raise the eyebrows of some pious sounding folk. I'm not telling you to drink and carry on, but I am saying that doing or not doing these things has nothing to do with being saved.

We know that an alcoholic drink can be deadly when drunk by some people. Alcohol has ruined lives. An alcoholic beverage can also be an enjoyable part of a good meal or gathering of friends.

Attending church can enrich a person's spiritual life and strengthen a family when the saints of God gather. However, attending church has also led to bitter quarrels and torn families apart when sin got the better of people in a congregation.

Salvation is a gift of God. It does not depend on what we do and don't do.

I've been avoiding Lutheran theological jargon. However, there is one piece of jargon I want to give you that I think you will find very helpful. (Just in case you think it might impress someone, the Latin term is *simul justus et peccator*. Although whom that will impress, I'm not sure.) Simultaneously saint and sinner, that's us!

If we are simultaneously saint and sinner, everything we do is contaminated by sin, but the saint in us is still up to a lot of good in spite of that sin.

Just like the people in the Bible

Whenever I really take a close look at the men and women described in the Bible, what really impresses me is how much like us they were. They were also this combination of saint and sinner.

Moses was a murderer. He also tried to talk God out of picking him to lead the children of Israel. He said he couldn't talk properly. Even though he was a great leader, he made a number of serious mistakes too.

We admire David's psalms and talk about what a great king he was. David was also an adulterer and a murderer and a poor father.

We know what a great mother Mary was. The way she obeyed God is very impressive. Mary also tried to stop Jesus' ministry when she thought he was getting carried away.

Peter was an impetuous guy whose mouth got him into a lot of trouble. Paul was a touchy, bossy sort of person. Mary Magdalene was not necessarily the kind of girl you would bring home to meet your mother. Thomas had many doubts.

God used every one of these people. The Bible also makes it clear that God loved every one of them. They didn't deserve that love any more than we do, but God loved them anyway. They are remembered as saints who struggled with sin and trusted in God.

Saints alive

I've talked so much about being a sinner that you might think that I'm really down on people. Not at all.

After all, as they say in Marriage Encounter, "God doesn't make junk."

Jesus said that we are to love God and to love our neighbors as ourselves. That means that we have to love ourselves. Jesus wouldn't have told us to love ourselves if he didn't believe that we are lovable.

We are simultaneously saint and sinner. Sometimes some people make it very hard for us to see the good in them. God never gives up on anyone, and God never writes anyone off. So we shouldn't write people off, especially ourselves.

Born again

You've probably heard someone talk about how Christians must be born again. Or someone might have asked you if you were a born-again Christian.

They got the term from a conversation recorded in John's gospel that Jesus had with Nicodemus. Jesus didn't use it anywhere else. Christians didn't pay much attention to it until the idea became popular at revival meetings in the last century or so.

Personally I think the term is an overworked cliché that should be avoided as much as any other cliché.

I didn't get any choice in being born. Lutheran doctrine teaches me that my faith is a gift of God. My rebirth in the waters of Holy Baptism is something that God willingly renews with me every day unless I am unwilling to accept God's grace. As I confess my sins and experience God's grace anew, I am born again and again and again and again.

The idea of being born again is usually associated with some deeply emotional conversion experience. For some Christians, God uses such experiences as an important turning point in their lives. The Apostle Paul represents the Bible's most dramatic story of conversion.

There are other Christians—such as Paul's student Timothy, and people like me—in whose lives the Holy Spirit is quietly present, leading us along a journey through life. Our experience of faith is seldom very dramatic. It is, nevertheless, equally important in set-

80

ting the direction for our lives.

The Bible

I've already talked a bit about how important the Bible is to us, but I haven't said much about why the Bible is so important. We believe that God inspired the people who wrote the Bible so that they could help us to learn the truth about God.

God didn't whisper in their ears and tell them exactly what to write and how. Their words reflect their personalities and styles and the times they lived in. The core of what the Bible has to tell us about God is the Gospel. Lutherans see everything in the Bible as centered in the good news of Jesus Christ.

The Bible is not one book. It is a collection of 66 pieces of writing. Although we call each one of these a book, they are really a collection of stories (such as Genesis, Ruth, or Mark), letters (such as Romans or Galatians), songs (such as the Psalms), wise sayings (such as the Proverbs) and prophecies (such as Isaiah or Jeremiah). Luther taught that they all had something important to teach us but the ones we should pay the most attention to are the ones that help us to understand God's grace.

Law and gospel

Martin Luther taught that the Bible deals with two basic categories: law and gospel. He believed that you had to understand the difference between the two before you could do any theology.

Luther taught that the law helps us to get along with each other. That's important. We can't murder each other or steal from each other or cheat and lie if we want to get along. God gives the law so that we have basic principles for taking care of each other, basic rules that are needed for a just society.

The law never does anything that helps to make us right with God. When it comes to salvation, Luther taught, all the law does is to show us how far from being perfect we are. When our actions are measured in the courts of heaven by the pure law of God and we are asked if we are sinners, we can do nothing but plead, "Guilty."

The gospel tells us that God decided to treat us as if we were not guilty, as if we were saints without any hint of sin, because God loves us. That's what we mean by God's grace freely given.

Gospel living is not a system of new rules and regulations. When we realize how much God loves us in spite of who we are and what we do, we can't help trusting God and returning God's love with love.

We don't do good to earn God's love. We try to do good because we know that God loves us and we want to please our gracious God.

The cross

Contrary to popular opinion Jesus' great commandment was not the Golden Rule: "Do unto others as you would have them do unto you." Jesus' great commandment was "Love one another as I have loved you."

Jesus proved his love for us by laying his life on the line, and that love cost him his life.

One of the people who taught me about reading the Bible once warned me saying, "Be careful what ideas you carry with you as you study the Bible. You will likely find all sorts of things to back up your idea if you look hard enough and long enough to find them. They won't necessarily be true to the gospel."

You can't talk about the gospel without running smack up against the cross. Jesus' cross teaches us that life with God isn't all sunshine and roses. There is pain and suffering and sacrifice involved when people trust God with their lives.

Just look what happened to Jesus. He wound up dying on that cross at Calvary.

There are Christians who come at the Bible with a different approach, sometimes called a theology of glory. They focus on the triumph of Jesus in the resurrection. They talk about how glorious life with God can be. Just follow Jesus and you will prosper, they claim. They don't tell the whole story.

The fruits of the Spirit, such as joy and peace and love, are part of a Christian's life, but so is taking up your cross and following Jesus. To avoid or ignore the cross is to avoid the way that Jesus calls us to travel.

I visited a woman in hospital who was dying of tuberculosis. At first she was quite hostile. "I don't believe in God," she said. "Don't try to convert me."

I explained that I was simply making myself available to talk about whatever she wanted to talk about. If she wanted, I would drop by to visit her whenever I was in the hospital. She said that she thought that would be all right.

To my horror I noticed that, on the wall by the woman's bed, one of the cleaning staff had hung a ghastly picture of Jesus dying on the cross. Since the woman didn't seem to object to it, I decided that I shouldn't mention it.

Our little visits were seldom more than friendly chats. One day she suddenly said to me, "You see that picture on my wall. I don't really understand it, and I'm still not what you would call a believer. But if there is a God like that, I know that he understands what I'm going through."

So what?

I've shared some pretty heavy stuff with you in this chapter. I haven't been able to do much more than skim over the surface of things. Still I hope that I have been able to give you some handles to help you work at doing some theology.

When you get right down to it, it doesn't matter what I say about God or what Martin Luther said or what anybody else has to say. Ultimately you have to decide for yourself what really matters to you.

The Spirit is walking with you and guiding you. God provides the Bible and the Church to help you to sort out what life with God is all about. In the end it is you who has to decide what this means.

Chapter 6

Photo: Kenn Ward

What we do with what we've got

Stewardship is everything we do after we say, "I believe." It's what we do with what we've got. Stewardship involves everything about us—our money, our time, our abilities. (We used to talk about "time, talent, and treasures," but for some reason or other, people tired of that trend.)

If stewardship is a word you don't know, it is one you need to learn. Stewardship is one of those words we use in church that you may not hear used very much anywhere else. When we want to talk about what we are doing with our lives, we have to talk about stewardship.

If I didn't hear stewardship mentioned in the congregation that I attend, I would begin to get worried. In a world that teaches people to ask, "What's in it for me?" stewardship reminds us that the world has a bad habit of asking the wrong questions.

Before I talk about what we do with what we've got, it's important for us to think about why we do what we do with what we've got. Got that?

Why we give

Christians regularly part with their hard-earned cash. They gladly give their time and share their ability. Why? Why would anyone want to give up their cash or their time?

If we sort out our motives first, then the rest starts to fall into place. God's grace, not greed or guilt, is why we give.

We don't do good in the belief that if we are good enough, then God will be good to us. We do good because God has **already** been good to us, and we want to share that goodness. It's so simple. But that point of view takes a lot of learning.

Some people think that their contributions are a way to grease God's palm. They think they can buy their way into heaven. They think that if you give enough or do enough for charity, God will be so impressed that your ticket to eternal bliss will be all arranged.

God can't be bribed. God doesn't need our charity. In fact God isn't running a charitable foundation. God is in charge of the whole universe.

That doesn't mean that God doesn't care about us or about what we do. The amazing thing is that the One who is in charge of the whole universe takes a personal, loving interest in us, each and every last one of us.

We do good because God's love for us brings out the goodness in us. We give because we want to, not because we have to.

The answer to my question at the beginning of this section is that we are not being asked to "give up" anything. We want to share what we have been given by God. People who give because they appreciate how rich God's love has made them, quickly learn that nothing is given up. In fact, a great deal is gained.

85

Money

When people talk about the value of something, they usually want to put a price tag on it. Most of us are smart enough to know that there are many valuable things in life that money can't buy, but big bucks sure do make an impression on us.

Some people talk about how much everything costs without any problem. Yet they have difficulty talking about money in church. It may be that they are suspicious of our motives. They may not realize that the church involves more than what they can see on Sunday morning and that it requires money to operate. They may simply be misinformed about what Christianity is really all about.

Or we may simply be getting too close to people whose hearts flutter with excitement when they hear rustling cash, but who start to stutter when it's "only" God's Word we want to share.

Let's be frank. People are also wary when church and money enter the same conversation because there are con artists who claim to be tending the flock when they are really out to fleece the faithful. These thieves not only steal people's money, they rob the real church of the trust it deserves.

Unfortunately, people may ignore a legitimate appeal because they've developed a habit of turning off any televangelist who asks for cash. The dishonest flim-flammers have alienated many people with their dishonesty, and it's hurt everyone.

That's why the ELCIC insists on proper financial record keeping at every level of our church. These records are regularly audited. Regular financial reports tell people where we get our money and how we spend it. This information is readily available to anyone so that they can check us out if they need to be sure that we can be trusted.

A down-to-earth faith

All this talk about money makes some people nervous. Shouldn't churches stick to spiritual things?

That way of thinking typifies many of the world's religions. These religions prefer to avoid "worldly" things like sex, money and politics. In their systems, if you become holy enough, sex, money, and politics don't interest you any more.

Jesus taught us that God is very interested in sex, money, and politics, because this is God's world. God gets involved in everything that goes on in this world.

Christianity is very materialistic. Our way of thinking about the world starts with Jesus. Jesus is God "incarnate," God "in the flesh." Rather than avoiding worldly things, God in Jesus jumped right into the thick of things. "God so loved the world..." the Bible tells us.

People who object to talking about money in the church haven't read the Bible. Jesus had no trouble talking about money. Neither did St. Paul. The Bible even suggests that one reason Jesus was crucified was because he threatened to ruin the way people had been making money at the Temple. Jesus challenged people to think about money and to question what really matters in life: "Where your treasure is, there your heart will be also." (Matthew 6:21 NRSV)

Experience has taught me that people are unwilling to open their wallets unless they have opened their hearts to God's love first.

How much should I give?

Sometimes people ask, "How much should I give?" If you've been paying attention, you know that I can't answer that question. There is no "should" to a Christian's giving.

In some European countries, where the Lutheran church is very strong, people contribute to the church as part of their taxes. In a sense the clergy are civil servants because they are paid by the government. Expenses for maintaining church buildings and programs also come from the church tax.

When these European Lutherans came to Canada, they found our voluntary system of offerings very confusing because giving had been automatic for them. They had to learn how to support church work in a country where Lutheranism was not the state church.

Some European Lutherans who arrived here since the Second World War still give very little to our congregations because they keep thinking that the money should come from taxes. However, they do give generously to overseas development and relief work because of their experiences. When many of them were refugees, they received help from such relief agencies in both postwar Europe and in getting settled in this country.

There was a time in the history of some of our congregations when each member was assessed a certain amount of money (a practice which may continue in places I am not aware of). This amount was expected to be given to the congregation as that member's fair share. It was treated like taxes, and a record of what each person gave was published. I believe that was a very poor way to encourage good stewardship. Although on the surface it seemed to be a fair and practical way of doing things, it forced people to give, not according to their ability, but according to what people would say if they didn't give.

I prefer what St. Paul had to say about giving when he wrote to the Christians in Corinth: "...if the eagerness is there, the gift is acceptable according to what one has..." (2 Corinthians 8:12 NRSV)

I've learned most of what I know about giving from studying what Paul has to say in chapter eight of his second letter to the Corinthians. I can't put it any better. So if you want to know more, get out your Bible and check out what Paul wrote.

Tithing

Some Christians give by tithing. This involves giving ten percent off the top for the work of God. The "tithe" is a biblical term. The Old Testament talks about people giving the first ten percent of their crops to God out of gratitude for the harvest.

I like the idea of the tithe, but I object to people who

try to make tithing into a rule. That takes the heart out of giving and turns it into a business transaction. Giving out of gratitude according to what God has given us is a much better principle. Measure your giving with your heart, not your calculator.

One man told me how he liked the idea of a tithe and felt that he should try to tithe. But he had children who needed an education. If he gave ten percent of his income, there wouldn't be enough for their education. I knew that he was not a careless spender and that he didn't earn much money.

I asked him, "Are your children part of your God-given responsibility?"

"Yes," he said.

"What do you think God would think of you if you didn't take care of those children?" I asked.

"I'll try to do the best I can for both God and my children," he said. "Maybe later on I can reach a tithe or even more than that."

My wife and I try to tithe. Sometimes we make it. Sometimes we go over. Sometimes other expenses get in the way. But we've managed to keep that goal in sight.

I'm glad we were challenged to consider tithing because that challenge forces us to look at how we plan to spend all of our money. After all, if you intend to take a certain percentage off the top, then you need to know how much you will have left and how much you need to live on.

Pledging

Pledging is a system of planned giving that many congregations find helpful. Before the year begins, members indicate in writing, on a form called a pledge card, the amount of money that they expect to be able to give to their congregation.

These pledges help the leadership of the congregation plan a budget. Because they know how much money they can expect, they can figure out how many different things they can do that year.

If you have already figured out a percentage of your

income which is feasible for you and which you want to give, it's very easy to fill in the card. You are just sharing with your congregation what you have already planned, so that they can make their plans.

Our congregations don't treat a pledge as a legal document, but it is something to consider carefully. People count on you to keep your word.

Sometimes the unexpected happens in our lives, and we are not able to meet our pledge. If that happens, it is important to let the congregation know so that adjustments can be made to their plans too.

Planning is the key here. Most people who say "I'll give what I can," really mean that they haven't planned on giving anything because they have never taken the time or trouble to think about planned giving.

Oh, they'll give, when they think of it, if anything happens to be left over. But they don't have a plan for how they will use their money. Such people usually aren't aware of their own priorities, and if they are, their priorities are on the wrong things, with church as an afterthought.

There are exceptions to anything. Self-employed or seasonally-employed people usually find it difficult to make a pledge because they often have no idea what they will earn. A few good members will not pledge as a matter of principle.

Such people are the exception. One source says that pledgers give three times as much in proportion to their incomes as those who don't pledge. Coincidence?

Envelopes

Using an offering envelope helps us to keep track of who gives what and where they want the money to go. Revenue Canada also requires churches to keep records so that receipts can be given for income tax purposes. It's a fact! The government actually gives you credit for giving to charitable purposes!

I like using envelopes for another reason. I can place my offering on the plate at worship without being self-conscious about the amount I am able to give. If I am able to be very generous, I can give quietly without notice.

Some people give post-dated cheques to their congregation as another way of doing the same thing. They also like this method because they know that they won't neglect the needs of their church even when they cannot attend every Sunday.

Some congregations use one envelope and divide the money between a variety of needs inside and outside the congregation according to whatever formula the congregation has chosen. Others have a list of causes on the envelope. They leave it up to you to fill in the amount that you want to go to each cause. Sometimes congregations use a special envelope for a special cause.

Personally, I prefer to just put the money in an envelope and trust the leadership to use it responsibly. Some causes are easy to give to. Other needs in the church don't get much publicity and aren't very glamorous, but they need our regular support too.

How it all adds up

I'm not going to give you a lot of figures, which you would probably skip anyway, about how synods and the ELCIC use the money they receive. One problem is that these figures change each year.

If you want to know exactly how every dollar and cent is spent in the ELCIC, you can get those figures at your local congregation. Every congregation has an annual report that includes financial records of how that congregation used its money. Each congregation also receives the "minutes" of the conventions of the synod and of the national church. These minutes include copies of the financial reports of the synod and of the national church respectively.

One trend that has been noted in many denominations, including the ELCIC, is that congregations tend to share less of their income with the synods and the national church than they used to. This may be a sign of the times—people think globally, but act locally. It may also be that churchgoers are not aware that membership in an ELCIC congregation involves a broader ministry than what they see on the local scene.

Spending the money

Most people have little idea where the money goes after it goes on the plate. They know that some of it pays the pastor's salary, maintains the building, buys necessary supplies and things like that.

They often don't realize that the money passed on to the synod and the national church also pays many salaries. Without benevolence giving from the congregations, there would be no money to pay for bishops, support staff, program staff, and the various directors. Those are only a few of the people who are affected.

Where do you suppose the money came from to train the pastor who stands in the pulpit? How do you think there happened to be Sunday school materials that could be ordered? Benevolence giving helped to make these things possible.

Giving to benevolence also helps the ELCIC to support missionaries and to develop new congregations. It makes campus ministry possible as well as church camping. It enables the ELCIC to work with other Canadian and world churches in matters of justice and peace, as well as evangelism.

This small list hasn't begun to exhaust the facets of ministry that benevolence giving makes possible. I hope I've given you enough for you to understand the important role each ELCIC congregation plays in making the total ministry of the synods and the national church possible. Without money from the local congregations, there would be no synod and no national church. It's as simple as that.

Democracy costs

Canada covers a lot of geography. It's expensive to bring people together for a meeting. But that's the price we pay to have as many people as possible involved in the decisions made by the ELCIC.

We could appear to be efficient and cut out many of the meetings that go on. That would cut down on costs, but it would also cut down on our effectiveness. Although two or three people could meet and make all the decisions for the church and it wouldn't cost much money, do you think the church could really afford **that** price?

When you don't agree

The ELCIC often faces difficult decisions regarding very controversial issues. Even after considerable debate, debate which allows as many people as possible to shape the final decision, no matter what is decided, there will always be those who do not agree with the decision. And what am **I** supposed to do when **I** don't agree with a decision the congregation, synod, or national church has made?

One practice I strongly oppose is that of withholding or cutting back on giving. In a democratic organization like the ELCIC, there are many, far more appropriate opportunities to make your views heard.

Voting with a cheque book is an irresponsible way to express your views. The cause being opposed is seldom affected. Instead, many valuable ministries are cut back due to lack of funds. Fortunately, this practice does not appear to be as strong in the ELCIC as it has been in some denominations.

On occasion, the church has made a decision that a person simply cannot support. The person can't ignore the decision, nor is it likely to be changed in the foreseeable future. Fortunately, because I have agreed with the decisions that our church has made, I have not been placed in that situation. But a few people have. Regrettably, they have decided to leave our denomination.

Time and ability

Everything I've said also applies to how we spend our time and how we use our ability. God gave each one of us specific abilities to build up the church.

I have yet to see a congregation that didn't have members with the talent it needed. I have seen congregations that weren't able to do their ministry because their members weren't putting their God-given ability to

work. I also know that there are times when an auto-
cratic pastor gets in the way of letting good lay people
do their jobs.

Even though our abilities may at times seem
meager, when they are recognized, appreciated, and put
to work God can do some wonderful things. I used to
visit a parishioner in a nursing home. She was blind,
almost deaf, and could barely walk. Yet she was a
cheerful soul who insisted on knowing the latest about
my children and my garden, even if I did have to shout
in her ear. She never complained and was grateful that
the staff would still take the time to help her walk a few
steps in the hall. She brightened the lives of everyone
she met through her simple faith.

Taking the time

There are no rules I can give you about how to use
your ability and time. I do have some suggestions.

I think every member should try to be involved in
one regular congregational activity beyond the Sunday
morning worship time. This might mean joining choir,
helping on a committee, serving on council, whatever.
Get involved in something that makes proper use of
your unique abilities.

But be very cautious about getting involved in more
than that. I'm not talking about helping with the occasional extra commitment that lasts for a short time. I
mean be careful of committing yourself to too many
regular things that require work month after month,
year after year.

Believe it or not, I believe that people can spend too
much time on church stuff. Over-involvement hurts the
church in two ways.

First, you may crowd someone else out of a job that
suits their talents perfectly. People never have a chance
to show what they can do if one or two people insist on
running the show.

Second, you might cut yourself off from the other
opportunities God has in mind for you outside the
church. Families have been deprived of time and love

that they badly needed from a family member who got too busy at church. Later on, embittered children or neglected spouses refuse to attend church because they feel that church robbed them of parent or partner.

Don't forget all the volunteer work in the community that needs willing workers. What was it that Jesus said about visiting the prisoner, the naked, the hungry, the sick? I don't remember him saying anything about leaving that ministry to the pastors.

If you have the time and the ability to get involved in the church beyond the congregation, jump at the chance. The rewards which come from involvement in the wider church far outweigh the work. That's where my own faith has been stretched, inspired, and challenged the most.

Making it work for us

I do a lot of ministry that is not in my job description. I'm neither bragging nor complaining. I do it willingly and gladly.

So do many other people. Because we feel that way, the ELCIC is able to do a lot more work than the dollars in its budgets would lead one to expect. That's because much of our work is done by volunteers.

Most people in the ELCIC are very dedicated. Too often we underestimate that dedication and don't ask them to give enough.

After one person gave a large amount to a particular campaign of the church, she was asked why she had never given that much before. "Well," she said, "nobody ever asked me before."

Just in case no one has ever asked you before, I'm asking you now. Please share your life generously in God's service. Stewardship is what we do with what we've got. Someone added to that a bit by saying that stewardship is what you do after you say, "I believe."

To quote Jesus again, "Where your treasure is, there your heart will be also." (Matthew 6:21 NRSV)

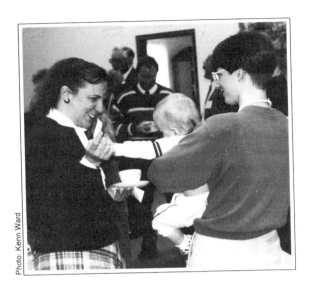

Photo: Kenn Ward

Sharing the good news

I remember a dance at our high school when I was in my early teens. The boys stood on one side of the gym and talked, nervously looking over at the girls who were standing on the other side of the gym doing the same thing.

There was one girl in particular who caught my eye. I kept looking over at her again and again, trying to work up the courage to ask her to dance with me. The evening was winding down. There were only a few dances left. I knew that if I didn't make my move, I would never get to dance with her that night.

Finally, with palms sweating and a mouth so dry that I was afraid that I would squeak when I spoke, I slowly and anxiously crossed the floor to where she stood. When I got there, I finally asked, "Will you dance with me?"—to the girl standing next to her.

I think that those feelings of anxiety and confusion just about sum up how most Lutherans feel about talking about their faith with other people. We know it's a good idea. We think it should come naturally. We even suspect that it might be a lot of fun if we could muster up the courage and go over there and say something. Much of the time we just think about it and somehow never cross the room.

It is not unusual for two Lutherans who attend different Lutheran churches to work together for many years, neither person knowing that the other is active in the Lutheran church. Then one day they will meet at a Lutheran gathering and greet each other, "I didn't know that you were Lutheran."

They weren't trying to keep it a secret. Talking about our church life, let alone our faith, is not something most Lutherans do very often.

In this chapter I'm going to suggest that talking about our faith is something Lutherans should consider doing more often. "Witness," "evangelism," "mission work..." Whatever label you want to stick on it, Christians are under orders from Jesus to go into all the world, teaching and preaching and baptizing.

Being offensive or going on the offensive?

Part of the reason that we don't say much about our faith is that we don't want to offend people. We like to be thought of as nice people—regular guys and gals who fit right in with the rest of the bunch. There's a lot of sage advice in that old saw that polite people don't talk about religion or politics; they stick to discussing the weather.

Let's face it. What Christians believe offends many people. Paul said, "...we proclaim Christ crucified, a stumbling block to Jews and foolishness to Gentiles." (1 Corinthians 1:23 NRSV). Paul could have added many other people to his list.

The Bible says that it is Jesus' way or no way. That

offends people who have put their faith in another way. Following Jesus' way means that we have to change our ways. Many people don't like to hear that kind of talk—unless their way isn't working out and they are searching for a better way.

Evangelistic styles

When we talk about evangelism, many of us think about rallies or crusades, events that run for several nights and have great musicians and a dynamic speaker. Most nights the place is packed. Some Lutherans love this form of evangelism. Others hate the idea.

I know people who have had their lives completely changed by such meetings. My own faith has been challenged and strengthened at such events. An important influence in my life has been the work and witness of the Anglican evangelist Marney Patterson.

Marney taught me not to write off anyone's attempt at evangelism, no matter how outrageous it might seem to me. What might look like nonsense to one person may be just the way that God reaches another person.

Marney tells of traveling with an evangelist in India. The evangelist took him for a ride in a car that had the back seat filled with single sheets of paper. Each piece of paper had a message about Christianity printed on it. "We're going to do some evangelism," the driver said. "Start throwing those papers out the window as we drive along."

Paper flew all over the road in the wake of the car. Marney was baffled.

"Look out the back window," said the driver. People were scurrying to pick up the papers and were reading them. "People here like to read but they don't have much opportunity," explained the driver. "We're giving them something to read. The seed we've planted will take root in some."

In Canada that would be called littering. Good Lutherans don't litter. But sometimes we **do** stick invitations to our worship services in people's mailboxes.

Doing and telling

While Lutherans sometimes help at rallies and crusades that involve several different church groups in a community, few of us really get involved in this kind of ministry. I wish we could catch some of that enthusiasm and dedication for sharing our faith with people who do not have a Christian faith.

I wish we could become more comfortable with telling other people about what we believe and why we believe it. (I don't mean speeches like the carefully rehearsed testimonials you see on TV religious talk shows, about how I was such a sinner and then I found Jesus and now everything is just wonderful.) If we don't practice talking about our faith, how are we going to be able to say the things that need saying when people ask questions?

One of my friends says that she never intentionally told anyone at work what Jesus meant to her. However, people generally knew of her commitment to the church through friendly conversation about "what happened on the weekend." Over the years a few asked the deeper questions. We need to be prepared for such moments.

We need to learn how to talk about what we believe and why we believe it in a way that doesn't insult anyone's intelligence. So often, people have prejudices based on stereotypes and caricatures of what church people are like. We have to find ways to approach these people, to let them learn what we are really like, to let them see that we are people much like themselves but with the resources of our faith.

Some people try to evangelize with methods that have more in common with slick-talking con artists than the people Jesus told us to be. That doesn't mean that the rest of us have to act that way.

Because we Lutherans are uncomfortable talking about our faith, we usually talk about our church rather than about Jesus. That's a good start, but eventually we have to explain to people why our church is important to us.

Some of us try to avoid this responsibility by claiming that we pay the pastor to talk about religion. We conveniently overlook the fact that the pastor isn't in our homes every day, has often never met our friends, and doesn't know the people where we work and play. The pastor seldom gets a chance to talk with those people. But we do.

Words and jargon

When people heard about the kind of language I was going to use to write this book, some of them said, "Finally! Someone is going to talk about religion using words that we can understand." Others said, "That doesn't sound very Lutheran to me."

To talk about our journey through life with God doesn't require any special words. The regular everyday words that we use to talk about most other things will do just fine.

Sure, there are special technical terms that theologians use when they practise their craft. However, as one theologian said, "When I'm caught between a rock and a hard place, I don't care about some existential reflection on God as the ground of our being. At times like that, words such as, 'Jesus loves me, this I know, for the Bible tells me so' or 'the Lord is my shepherd' are what I want to hear."

Nor do you have to memorize some formula for witnessing that spells out just the right questions in just the right order with just the right answers. Witnessing is not like producing widgets on an assembly line.

In fact, a memorized spiel will likely drive away the person you are talking to because it's artificial and contrived. Real people want to hear from other real people, people who can share experiences of faith, not canned religious jargon. We are not doing a sales job on these people; we are sharing the stuff of life that is most important to us.

One of Luther's favorite questions was, "What does this mean?" His students quickly learned that the question demands more than a memorized answer from the catechism.

One to one

A good way to witness to our faith is to talk about it with the people we meet every day. I do not mean that we should walk up to everyone we meet, look them in the eye, and ask, "Are you saved?" However, if faith is an important part of our lives, then it should naturally be part of all the other things that we talk about with people.

Witness takes place when a family eats a meal together, when we have coffee with a friend, when we are at work or at play, doing our shopping, or visiting a sick friend.

One of my favorite evangelists is the girl I mentioned in an earlier chapter, the one who was her father's sponsor at his baptism. That event took place because of a walk she took with her parents in their neighborhood several years before.

They happened to walk by a church and she asked her mom and dad, "What's that building?"

"It's a church," they said.

"What's a church?" she asked.

"Well, we're not exactly sure because we don't go to church," they said.

"Can we go and see?" she asked.

It's that simple and that profound. If only we could learn to be as natural as children.

The caring community

Al Evans was a United Church chaplain at the university I attended. He had a habit of coming up and asking, "How are things?" Before you knew it, you were telling him all about whatever happened to be bothering you at the time.

There are many hurting people around us who need someone to listen to their hurts. My wife, Diane, is much better at this than I am. She can be standing in line at the grocery store or at a bus stop and the next thing I know some total stranger is telling her their life story.

Knowing just the right thing to do or say seems to come naturally to her. I am learning how to help others with their hurts because Diane, and other people in my life like her, have helped me with my hurts.

When I was a parish pastor, I had a team of special evangelists although none of them knew that they were part of a team. If I knew that someone was hurting, I would suggest to another member who I knew would understand, "Why don't you get together with so-and-so? I think they need someone to talk to."

One very shy lady used to slip out after service as quickly as she could. She came from another country and carried several heavy burdens in her life. There was another woman from her homeland who also had similar burdens but who had been able to draw on the resources of her faith for strength.

I told the second woman about the first one and suggested that she try to become friends with her. It wasn't long before I would usually see the two of them in friendly conversation after the service.

Another way to help people talk about their faith is to have them share stories about their lives in a small group. It could be a story about why I came to this church, or about the person who has most influenced my life, or even about my favorite time of the day.

As people share their stories, they begin to know each other. Bonds of trust are built. In such conversations, God can be talked about as a natural part of the rest of the story.

At one of these storytelling sessions, a man in our congregation told us about why he was part of our congregation and about how much his membership meant to him. He talked about how his faith gave him strength to face his job. He shared a bit about what prayer meant to him.

When he finished, his wife turned to him and said, "I never knew any of that. All these years I thought you came to church just because I dragged you along."

Sharing stories

Evangelism involves sharing the story of my life with God. As I tell you my story, I hope that you will begin to realize that **your** story is an important part of God's story too. You probably won't believe that what I'm saying is really part of my life unless I can talk with you about it the way I talk with you about everything else.

Before I begin to share my story, I have to really listen to what the other person has to share with me. A very important part of storytelling is wanting to hear the other person's story.

Personally, I find that hard to do. One time Diane even hung up a sign by my telephone that read, "Remember. God gave you two ears and only one mouth."

A good evangelist must be a good listener. Where are the hurts and the joys in this person's life? If you have had similar experiences, how has your faith enriched or helped you with them?

That's the way Jesus talked about faith. He was "tuned-in" to the lives of the people around him. He used simple stories from the lives of those people.

He saw some shepherds with their sheep, and he explained how God cares for people the way those shepherds looked after their sheep. He saw a woman searching for a lost coin. He said that God searches for lost souls in the same way. More than that, God is happier about a lost soul being found than that woman was about finding her lost coin.

A minority group

Some people are upset by the idea that Canada cannot be considered a "Christian" country any more. I'm not sure that Canada ever **was** a Christian country, although many once took the idea for granted.

In the past, people claimed that the things they did were based on Christian principles. A closer look calls a lot of those claims into question. Now that the law of the land does not enforce Christian-based principles, we find that many people don't really care about those principles.

There was a time, within the memory of our older members, when most people went to church regularly. Those who didn't felt it necessary to apologize for not going, or to explain why they didn't go. The church was one of the most important parts of a community's life. It was important to attend because that's where the action was. Not any more.

One businessman told me that when he and his wife became active in their church, they began to have less and less in common with their former circle of friends and acquaintances. He is not the kind of person who would ram religion down anyone's throat, but he is also not a man who is silent about his faith.

As the years passed, he noticed that he and his wife had developed an entirely new circle of friends, all of whom were also active in the church. "Our former friends don't understand how we can spend so much time with church people," he said. "You know something? We really have a good time with our Christian friends. In fact, we have more fun now than we ever did."

In Canada, Christians who are actively involved in the life of a congregation and who try to practise the things that they preach and teach are a minority group. Most people in Canada no longer share a common experience with us. They don't know the Bible's stories, and they probably don't care.

Digging out the answers

This means that when we take a stand, we may not have much company. Life is full of choices. As Christians, we are asked to make choices that other people may not understand or agree with.

Your sister and her new husband fly in to spend a holiday weekend with you. She doesn't go to church any more and he never did. Do you skip going to service that Sunday? Or do you invite them along and maybe face refusal, ridicule, or some pointed questions that you hadn't really thought about?

Why do we need churches? Why is church important to you? The answers may not be as simple or as obvious as you think.

It isn't just individuals who ask these kinds of questions. Entire congregations and denominations ask them. One of the most pressing questions facing the

ELCIC concerns its mission in Canada.

The ELCIC has traditionally been made up of immigrants—immigrants who were Lutheran. But times have changed. Do we now focus our attention on immigrants who aren't even Christian? Or do we concentrate on the generation of children in our congregations who are drifting away from church? Or should we try to do both?

We have a strong tradition of teaching, and our liturgy has been important to our identity. Still, many of our own members do not understand our traditions. Do we turn inward and rediscover who we are before we invite others to join us? Or do we modify or ignore our traditions so that we can get on with telling our story to whomever we can find who will listen?

Sociologists such as Reginald Bibby tell us that people who are looking for a church act like people in a shopping mall. If you don't know how to market your product with the packaging that consumers want, they won't buy what you have to sell. Should we work to make our "package" more attractive? Should we work at being more hospitable and "user-friendly"? Or should we refuse that thinking and insist that what is important is not what **we** want, but what **God** wants? And what exactly **does** God want?

To get at answers to those kinds of questions, some congregations hold study sessions, or weekend retreats, or bring in a special consultant to help them to talk about who they are and what they want to become. When all the talking is over, sometimes they end up with what is called a "mission statement."

The mission statement says "This is who we are and this is where we intend to go." It helps the congregation to do some long-range planning and gives people a sense of direction when they begin to wander off course.

Different approaches

I've seen congregations that were aimlessly drifting along develop a mission statement and then do some ministry that really amazed them. Several have become very active in the life of their community. They have built special housing to improve conditions in their neighborhoods, or opened a food bank, or begun a counseling service or a daycare center. Others have revised the way they worship and have developed ways to invite new people in and to help them to become a real and active part of their growing ministry.

What works for congregations might be good for each one of us. I haven't tried to write a personal "mission statement" but it might be a good idea. At its most basic, it might say something like "I intend to be a faithful member of Messiah Lutheran Church in Winnipeg, so that I can worship, learn, witness and serve in the ways to which the other members and I feel God is calling us."

The national church

We have a few formal strategies in the ELCIC for witnessing. We have two divisions of the church fully devoted to this work: the Division for World Mission, and the Division for Canadian Mission. Our Division for Colleges and University Services devotes part of its energy to providing a witness on campuses, while our Division for Church and Society helps us to act on our faith as a public witness to the ethical and social values that are part of being Christian.

You will find a few of us in foreign countries serving as pastors, teachers, health-care workers, agricultural and industrial advisers, and helping with community development. Forget your stereotypes about missionaries. Most missionaries never thought or acted the way you've seen them depicted in the movies.

Should missionaries stay home?

Critics have recently accused mission work of being nothing more than an extension of imperialism. This happens because people get confused about the difference between Christendom and Christianity.

Christendom describes the social order that resulted when the Roman emperor Constantine converted to Christianity in the fourth century. Christianity became the official religion of the Roman Empire. This brought all sorts of privileges and powers, which had little to do with Christianity, to the church. Christianity has never been seen in quite the same way since.

Shameful things have been done in the name of Christ over the centuries that reflect Christendom rather than Christianity. Rulers of "Christian" countries waged war on "pagan" countries and claimed that God was on their side. Jews have long been a target of bigotry and prejudice by some Christians who were manipulated more by political and economic forces than by religious reasons. Nor can we be proud of Christendom's historical relationship with the Muslim world. Christendom has much to repent.

When the imperial forces of countries like Spain, Portugal, Holland, Germany, England, and France set out to conquer foreign lands, they took their faith with them. This faith was a blend of Christendom and Christianity. Few of them would have understood the distinction between the two.

For example, a British missionary might sincerely believe that British codes, culture and customs were as much a part of being a "real" Christian as were the teachings of the Bible. They would also have been deeply offended if someone had questioned their codes, culture or customs on the basis of the Bible.

Modern Christians must be aware of the difference between Christendom and Christianity. The job of a true missionary is not to get people to adopt the ways of the missionary's country—whether those "ways" involve capitalism, imperialism, communism, or any other "ism."

Missionaries share the good news about Jesus and his way of love, truth, and mercy. If you check the real record of most missionaries, you will find that they have helped people to improve their lives through education, health care and other practical things. At the heart of what they shared was the conviction that each person is a child of God, a child whom God considers worth loving and for whom there is hope and dignity as God intended.

Missionaries often get into trouble in foreign countries

these days. Not because they are guilty of cultural imperialism, but because they share the Christian message about the way that God wants us to live together. This message threatens the people in power who prefer that their abuse of power not be called into question.

Ironically, Canada has also become a mission field. Christians from other countries now come here to proclaim the gospel. A number of our newest mission congregations reach out to new immigrants such as Chinese-speaking people. The pastors who serve these congregations are immigrants themselves.

Deeper answers

Lutherans have not always been quick to question those in power, even though this is also part of our witness. Most of us still don't like to challenge the status quo. While some Canadian churches have a history of asking the tough questions about social conditions, this is still something fairly new for Canadian Lutherans.

We were often new immigrants who spoke the language haltingly. We were busy getting our farms going, or working hard at low-paying jobs just to get a start in a new country. We stuck with our own kind. We didn't have time for politics. Besides, those people in politics were mainly Roman Catholics, or Anglicans, or Presbyterians, and we knew that those people really weren't interested in what we had to say.

Over time we began to find our voice, and we discovered that those other Christians were willing to share power with us. They even wanted to work with us. So we also began to ask probing questions, and we haven't been very satisfied with the answers we've been getting.

You don't have to ask too many questions about the way things are done in this country, or the way the international community works, before you realize that there is a gap between the rich and the poor. In Canada, most of us receive the basic necessities but the gap between rich and poor is growing.

However, when you compare what we in this country have with what others in the so-called Third World or the South have, you begin to realize that the gap is a chasm that is growing, and that the economic policies of nations like ours are part of the cause.

As people in the Third World begin to analyze the causes of this growing chasm, we find ourselves confronted with a credibility gap. When privileged Canadians go to Third World countries to share their faith, they discover that economic actions speak louder than pious words.

Biblical politics

There are those in the Lutheran church who sincerely believe that what I've just been talking about has nothing to do with witnessing to our faith. They say things like, "Forget all this political stuff and stick to the Bible."

It does help to stick to the Bible. One of the clearest messages that I have found in the Bible reads, "what does the Lord require of you but to do justice, and to love kindness, and to walk humbly with your God?" (Micah 6:8 NRSV)

Forgive me if I sound as if I've climbed onto a soap box. One of my deepest convictions is that faith cannot be tucked away in a little compartment of our lives labeled "religious stuff." Our faith affects every part of our lives, or it is not faith. If we believe that this is God's world, then how can people of God say that they have no business talking about what God wants for this world?

In this society, we back up our beliefs with our chequebooks and our appointment books. We spend our money on the things that we think are important. If you want to know what I really believe in, take a look at the way I spend my money and how I spend my time.

In many congregations, when a person is baptized, we take a candle and light it from the Christ candle. Then we hand it to the newly baptized person while repeating Jesus' words, "Let your light shine before others that they may see your good works and give glory to your Father in heaven."

109

Does the love of God shine through when we open our wallets and when we open our mouths?

None of what I've said means that Christians have all the answers when it comes to solving political issues and matters of justice. In fact our solutions may not be any better than anyone else's, and some of our plans may be very naive or totally impracticable.

Politicians and economists are special people with special gifts. It is not the church's responsibility to do their job for them. However, it is the church's responsibility to remind them (and all of us as citizens) of basic biblical principles when they do their jobs.

It doesn't matter whether or not they believe in God. It doesn't matter whether they are willing to listen to us or not. It does matter that we have given a faithful public witness.

Taking a stand

Christians say that Jesus is Lord. That declaration shook the entire Roman Empire and changed the course of history. As you will learn in the chapter "All in the family," when Luther took his stand at Worms, it not only changed the face of religion in Europe, it affected the entire political structure of Europe.

Many people are aware that, during the Second World War, a number of Lutherans in Germany followed Adolf Hitler (so did German Roman Catholics). Only a few, such as Dietrich Bonhoeffer, dared to question or to disobey.

The war record of Scandinavian Lutherans is less well known. The Nazis insisted that all Jews pin a triangle to their clothing so that they could be identified. In Denmark, a country where most people are Lutherans, King Christian pinned a triangle to his clothing and asked every citizen to do what he had done. Most people did so.

There are many stories of the courage of individuals and small groups of people of faith. Still, if more people had been willing to take a public stand for their faith, history may have been written quite differently.

TV or not TV

When I use the word evangelist, you probably form a picture in your mind of some person on TV who flashes a big toothy smile at the camera, who talks a lot about "Jesus, Jesus, Jesus," and who asks you to send cash, cash, cash.

Religious con artists are all too real. They take advantage of the inherent good in religion and give real people of faith a bad reputation. Unfortunately, there are many "religious" programs on TV that should inspire nothing more than an itchy finger on the channel changer. Some of them are dangerous to your mental health and destroy Christianity's credibility with people who have any intelligence.

There are notable exceptions. Some denominations and media ministries try to use TV intelligently to share the faith with those too timid to walk into a church.

Some Lutherans would like to be part of more of this kind of television and have done programs with the CBC and Vision TV. However, this work is very expensive. So what we've been able to do thus far is very limited.

While our worship services are not intended to be a media event, some of our congregations broadcast their Sunday morning worship service over the radio or on TV. Most of the audience are people who for one reason or another can't make it out to church. This ministry helps them to feel connected to the people of God. Occasionally the service touches someone who happened to turn it on and left it on out of curiosity. They have discovered a faith they had been missing.

The printed word

Lutherans love to write. Much of what we write is published by Augsburg Fortress in the United States and is distributed by Augsburg Fortress Canada in Kitchener, Ontario, and Calgary, Alberta. You can find a number of these books in other bookstores across Canada too.

Many people think that Wood Lake Books, which published this book, somehow belongs to the United

Church of Canada. It is actually an independent business that has no formal ties with any church. However,
many churches in Canada, including the ELCIC, are
beginning to find that Wood Lake has a special style
that Canadians like to read, and it has the ability to
help Christian writers in Canada get their words into
print. This book would not have happened without the
initiative of Jim Taylor at Wood Lake.

Before the ELCIC was formed, Lutherans in Canada
pretty much left writing to American Lutherans and
bought the things that they wrote. A notable exception
was Concord Canada which was operated by the Evangelical Lutheran Church **of** Canada and which published the work of a few Canadian Lutherans. Since the
formation of the ELCIC, we have worked to encourage
more of our own people to develop their writing skills.
We have discovered some pretty good writers with ideas
well worth reading.

The main place where ELCIC members share their
ideas in print is *Canada Lutheran*, the magazine of
which I'm editor. The magazine records the history of
the ELCIC as it happens. It tells who we are and what
we believe. It highlights the issues we debate, as well as
our celebrations, our frustrations, and our triumphs.

Evangelical Lutheran Women produce a gem called
Esprit. The magazine recently won an award from the
Canadian Church Press which referred to it as "a bright
light in the sometimes dreary world of religious publishing."

People interested in theology may want to read
Consensus, A Canadian Lutheran Journal of Theology,
sponsored by Lutheran Theological Seminary and
Waterloo Lutheran Seminary.

People concerned about social issues might consider
a subscription to *Praxis*, published by the Institute for
Christian Ethics at Waterloo Lutheran Seminary.

Start spreading the news

We haven't had much practice talking and writing
about our faith. Nor have we made many films or videos

that help people to get a glimpse of our faith in action. At last count, there were more than 206,000 stories just waiting to be told. (That's about how many baptized members we have.)

We need to do more of these kinds of things. We have a lot of good news to share in a world weighed down by bad news. As resources become available, the ELCIC will likely produce many more pamphlets and books and videos and tapes and magazine articles and the like. That's good.

The Holy Spirit helps us to share God's good news in many ways. But one of the best ways to share the faith begins with, "Hi! How are things?"

Chapter 8

Photo: Ferdy Baglo

Living what we believe

I had just moved into town. I was invited to a meeting of the local ministerial association. A couple of the ministers were trying to persuade the others that the churches in town should start a petition to have the local tavern's liquor license removed.

"Why would you want to do that?" I blurted out, quite surprised at the suggestion. "It's the only place in town where a person can get a drink!"

I quickly discovered that there were two distinct views about what was and what was not Christian in that town, and that my Christianity was very suspect by some of the other clergy.

We had some serious differences of opinion about how morality gets played out in public policy. Many

Lutherans, particularly those who know their theology, get nervous when people try to legislate their view of morality, even if we happen to agree with the moral point being made.

The two sides of morality

Our moral point of view affects what we do both publicly and privately. Sometimes people get upset when the church talks about these things. What the church says may call some of their own behavior into question or challenge a firmly held idea or opinion.

Some people expect the church to have very clear and firm rules about things like who sleeps with whom, abortion, divorce, or picking somebody's pocket. Other people want the church to speak up about corporate rip-offs and corruption in high places.

Sometimes the people who worry about personal morality think the church shouldn't get involved with society's ills. They would be very upset that the company's vice-president in charge of quality control slept with someone else's husband. At the same time, they might merely shrug if told that she placed a potentially unsafe product on the market because skipping the testing meant bigger profits for her shareholders.

And sometimes the people who think that the church should speak out about pollution and politics think that the church shouldn't get in such a huff about personal sins. They're willing to be dragged off to jail in protest over logging rights, but will look the other way if one of their friends sniffs cocaine.

You can find Lutherans who match both of the descriptions I've just given. Traditionally, social or personal morality has not been a very big part of the Lutheran agenda.

When we do take a public stand, we are quick to point out that we are not trying to give the ultimate answer that will stand forever. We are trying to do what is right as faithfully as we can. Everything we do is an act of faith.

At best, all we can do is say that we have given this

matter serious consideration, and this is the best we can come up with at this time. We may find a better, more complete answer at some time in the future. We do our best and trust God with the rest.

Taking care of business

Remember, we Lutherans had quite a bit of history behind us before we came to this country. When the Lutheran church got its start in Germany and Scandinavia, the nations of Europe were just getting started. The Lutheran church played an important part in that process. The rulers of these emerging nations and the Lutheran church leaders worked together. The Lutheran church was part of the establishment, just as the Anglican church was part of the English establishment.

Martin Luther was very conservative when it came to politics, and he supported the status quo. He taught that God looks after what goes on in the world in two very distinct ways.

This theory is called the "two kingdoms" or "two realms" theory. Luther developed it at a time when there was still a rigid feudal system in Germany and everyone was still sure of their place in the scheme of things. In our day, the distinctions between rulers and the ruled are not as clear-cut as they were in Luther's time.

Some Lutherans feel that the two kingdoms theory is simply a great way to justify the status quo. However, Lutheran theologians still find the distinctions helpful as we try to sort out moral and social issues. According to this theory, we should not get the business of the one realm (the government) confused with the business of the other realm (the church). Here's the way it is supposed to work out.

The government's business

According to the two kingdoms theory, God provides governments for basic social order. The business of government is justice, and the government may use force, if necessary, to make people obey. Government is a complex business. Lutherans recognize that many

116

compromises must happen to make it work.

Lutherans do not expect governments to be "Christian" nor do they try to "Christianize" them. Good laws don't make people good. But they may make how we live together a bit better for everyone.

The church's business

On the other side of the two kingdoms theory, God provides the church to proclaim the gospel. The church's "business" is to share God's grace. It may call people to become God's people, but it cannot force them to be loving and forgiving.

In practice things don't work out that neat and tidy, and modern-day Lutherans aren't really sure that this two kingdoms theory is as good as it could be. However, it still has a lot of influence on the way we think about morals—public and private—even if we aren't all that aware of why we think the way we do.

Facing the hard questions

As the editor of a church magazine, I regularly receive letters from irate readers who claim that something I have published is bound to lead people straight to hell. Whenever I get one of these letters, I realize that someone's sense of piety (or idolatry?) has been offended.

Such people usually write out of deeply held convictions and can quote chapter and verse from parts of the Bible that they believe support their views. I find that their letters are usually more concerned with laying down the law than learning what it means to be a loving child of God.

What is the loving thing to do? That's a tough question to answer.

Good parents know that letting your children do whatever they want is not loving. Sometimes to teach our children how to behave properly, we have to restrict them and even use strong discipline to keep them from hurting themselves and others.

Nor does the Bible take immoral behavior lightly. Our sins have serious consequences that affect many people. So we cannot remain silent and simply let people do whatever they please.

Why we take a public stand

Early in its life, the ELCIC discovered that there are times when it is expected to take a stand on matters of morality and ethics. So it said that whenever it did so, it recognized that social ethics are filled with paradox and ambiguity.

The ELCIC uses its Public Statements for three purposes. They are an opportunity to teach people and to help them understand the issues. They guide the ELCIC in looking at how the ELCIC itself does things. In other words, do we practice what we preach? They also provide some guidance and support for individual Christians who live with the situations described in the statements and who may have to make decisions concerning these issues.

If you want to go into this in more detail, you should write to the ELCIC Division for Church and Society. Ask for "The Public Witness of The Evangelical Lutheran Church in Canada."

So where do we stand?

Most of the material that exists in print about various social issues was written before the ELCIC began. These documents were developed by the groups who formed the ELCIC. If the ELCIC has not made its own statement about the matter, we still refer to what was said by those Lutherans before we became the ELCIC.

Here are a few words about some of the things people usually wonder about when they ask "Where does the Lutheran church stand?" Keep in mind that this is not the last word on the subject. It is simply a quick run-through in alphabetical order of 19 issues which I think you may be wondering about.

Abortion

The ELCIC's position on abortion is to encourage a type of society in which people will no longer feel that abortion is necessary or desirable.

We must become a more loving and just society if we expect to eliminate abortion. We often refuse to admit that poverty and abuse are important factors in why women get pregnant and why they feel that they need an abortion. Too often, we do little to provide any real help or support for people who struggle with difficult choices in their lives.

The ELCIC wrestled with the matter for many years, and we finally approved "Stewards of Creation: Respect for Human Life" at the 1991 ELCIC Convention. There is a vocal minority in the ELCIC who feel that the ELCIC should state its opposition to abortion more clearly. For them, abortion is killing, plain and simple.

Abuse

Along with the rest of Canadian society, the ELCIC has been very slow to come to grips with the reality of abuse. Even now, when it is becoming obvious that many of our members have suffered abuse at the hands of family members, friends, and even from some of our clergy, we still tend to avoid the matter.

An important reason for this slowness is that the victims of abuse are usually women, children, and the elderly, while the power in the ELCIC has rested in the hands of men. (My use of that image is not accidental.) Some men, more men than we care to admit, have abused that power. It remains to be seen what measures the ELCIC will take to change the way its structures operate so that it does not reinforce situations that encourage abuse.

Addictions

We haven't really come to grips with addictions any better than the rest of society. We are concerned about hard drugs, but we are aware that the abuse of prescription drugs by our members is also a serious problem. So are other addictions such as workaholism, gambling, and compulsive shopping.

Caring communities of supportive Christians can

help addicted persons to overcome their addiction. Some congregations provide such support. Others hesitate even to admit that members among them are addicted.

Most Lutherans have come to realize that smoking is a health hazard both to smokers and to those around them. When I attended my first synod conventions, there were ash trays on the tables. Now it is a matter of policy that ELCIC headquarters in Winnipeg is a smoke-free work place. This is also the policy of most ELCIC congregations.

Lutherans are divided on their opinion about the use of alcohol as a social beverage. Some members of a few ELCIC congregations oppose the use of alcohol. They may use grape juice for Holy Communion as part of their commitment to a deeply held conviction. In other congregations, wine and cheese parties may be part of congregational life.

My personal policy is that it is okay to have a drink as long as the drink doesn't have you. Many other Lutherans share this view.

However, the abuse of alcohol is a serious social problem. Many congregations open their doors to groups such as Alcoholics Anonymous, Al-Anon, or Alateen.

Ageism

I didn't think much about ageism until an older man in a congregation that I was serving became quite angry about something that I had said. When I started to talk with him about it, he suddenly snapped, "Why should we talk about this? You never take me seriously anyway."

I was shocked. The man was an important leader in the congregation. As we talked, I discovered that some of the things that I said at meetings, and the way I treated him, had left the impression that I thought he was an old fool.

I really had a great deal of respect for the man and his judgment, but I began to realize that I had been allowing a sense of ageism to cloud my attitudes and actions. We straightened things out between us, and my respect for him deepened.

Retired people may be one of the church's greatest blessings. They have a wealth of experience. Some find retirement provides a chance to work on projects for their church that they never had time to take on before.

However, as a 1978 Lutheran statement observed, "They are forced too readily into retirement, often eased out of responsible leadership positions in the church and community, too frequently 'protected' from making life-affecting decisions and in some instances made the objects of service activities that other well-meaning persons plan and administer."

Caring for creation

I doubt that I have to convince you that ecology and taking care of the environment are important. Things weren't like that in 1972 when Lutherans were among the few who were talking about the ecology. A 1972 statement of the Lutheran church had to provide a definition of the word "ecology" because few had ever heard it used.

Unfortunately, although we had our definitions straight and we provided some sound theological reasons why it was important to take care of the planet, we did not put theory into practice. We've been as slow as everyone else in learning the three r's: reduce, reuse, recycle.

As we build new churches, we pay more attention to energy conservation, and we renovate older buildings with better technology. Disposable dishes are disappearing from church functions. Some of our conventions even ask delegates to bring their own coffee mugs.

However, we are still major consumers of paper. The amount of paper we use for reports and records and Sunday services, which get a quick glance and then end up in the garbage, is staggering. We are turning to recycled paper and recycling what we can. But we still have a lot to think about in this area.

Censorship

More and more people are alarmed by what comes into their homes through their television sets. Murder and mayhem are part of many young children's daily viewing diets. Violence, vulgar language, and scenes of sex in the nude suddenly appear at the flick of a switch.

While the ELCIC has not looked into the issue in an official way, other than sharing in a recent ecumenical statement on pornography, a 1978 Lutheran statement which talks about human rights says that, "No one has the right to debase sexuality by abstracting it from personal relationship, by making it a commodity for consumption, or by using it as a commercial inducement."

Crime and punishment

According to a 1972 statement, when a crime is committed, the response should emphasize helping the offender learn to live in society rather than punishment and imprisonment. Community service and restitution could be part of such sentences. Jail should be limited to offenders who are judged dangerous or violent.

Reconciliation rather than retribution is emphasized. This emphasis is motivated by grace rather than fear.

The statement also says that we often try to make scapegoats out of the people we appoint to administer justice—police, judges, prison guards, parole officers and the like—instead of giving them the resources they need to do their jobs.

It is easier to blame the cops for not being tough enough on criminals when a violent shooting takes place than to ask why the person had a gun or what caused the violence. Why, for example, are most offenders young men from lower income families? Why are so many of Canada's native people in prison—a proportion far out of line with their numbers in society?

The ELCIC opposes capital punishment and supports the decision of Parliament to abolish capital punishment in Canada.

A number of our members disagree with the ELCIC's position and with the decision of Parliament. The fear of violence often pushes people to see punishment as the only response to crime. However, violence (including violent punishment) simply encourages more violence.

122

The ELCIC belongs to the Church Council on Justice and Corrections as a way to work on these issues. A number of Lutheran pastors also serve as chaplains at provincial or federal correctional institutions.

Divorce

The ELCIC does not support divorce, but it does support those who have been divorced. It is not enough to say that divorce and remarriage are not what God intended, or to quote what Jesus said about divorce. We also know that God loves and accepts us even when we sin, and that God deals with us according to our needs. People **do** get divorced, and they need support.

I conducted a survey about divorce in one parish I served. Every person in that parish had been directly touched by divorce. Either he or she was divorced, or was a close family member of someone who had been divorced.

Far too many people in our society marry the wrong person for the wrong reasons. Eventually they discover their tragic mistake. Sometimes a bad marriage can be turned around with a lot of hard work. But there are times when the best solution is to separate two people who should not be married to each other.

Reader response to draft copies of this book told me that a lot more needs to be said about this subject. This concern tells me that congregations should consider seriously their ministry to these people.

Economic justice

I'll bet that this issue wasn't on the tip of your tongue. But it has bothered Lutherans for a long time.

We haven't found many answers. But we continue to press the questions whenever governments start talking about things such as housing, education, social services, employment standards, job creation, and trade policy.

Christians say that this is God's world. We are created in God's image and given the responsibility to care for this earth and to share its blessings.

How do we do that in a way that is fair for everyone, so that everyone has an equal opportunity; so that people can be called to account for what they do, so that what we do does not waste our resources?

Euthanasia

While the ELCIC does not support the use of heroic measures to preserve life when such action will not have any real value, deliberately helping a person to commit suicide is another matter. As Christians, we have a responsibility to treasure and preserve the life which God has given us, whether that is our own life or another person's life.

When a person is terminally ill and no cure is available, we still have the responsibility to care for that person so that life may be lived to the fullest until death takes place. From personal experience, I know that giving such care has taught me to value life more than ever. Some "hopeless cases" have turned out to be people who taught me important lessons in hope and faith.

Gambling

Back in 1965, a convention of Lutherans said that gambling was wrong. Very few people paid much attention.

If you asked for a show of hands in most Lutheran congregations, you would likely discover several people who had recently purchased a lottery ticket, or played bingo, or taken part in a raffle. Most would probably tell you that it was for a worthy cause.

The 1965 Statement on Lotteries said that gambling caters to our selfishness and feeds on the covetousness that is forbidden in the Ten Commandments. It denies our social responsibility by encouraging us to take from our neighbors instead of taking on the **needs** of our neighbors. (We'd rather buy lottery tickets and convince ourselves that it helps charities and hospitals and recreation, than support a fair tax system that ensures that these needs are met.)

Many church people are only beginning to realize

that they should have paid more attention to what was said in 1965.

Health care

A number of institutions and agencies related to the ELCIC across the country provide direct care, particularly care for the elderly. This reflects the tradition of the Christian church which has included healing as part of its ministry since Jesus' time.

Canadians have excellent health care because caring Lutherans spoke and worked for a system that protected all of Canada's citizens. Our 1969 statement "Towards Adequate Health Care for all Canadians" has been widely used to interpret medicare.

The ELCIC is concerned about the erosion of the comprehensive health-care system with which Canada has been blessed for several decades. It supports universally accessible health care as a right of every citizen. Lutherans in Canada have taken a leading role in advocating universal, accessible, portable, comprehensive health care under public administration. Canada cannot be a healthy nation if it does not take care of the health of its citizens.

Homosexuality

Homosexuality is one of the hottest subjects facing denominations at the moment. The subject has become so politicized that it is hard to get people to sit down and discuss things in a rational way. We have not yet found ways to trust each other enough to get beyond our emotions. Understandably, those among us who are homosexual doubt that it is safe to come out of the closet.

One person who tried to foster dialogue about homosexuality was accused of being a moral coward for insisting that he wanted to keep an open mind until he had more information. He discovered a book that presented some scientific research into homosexuality that he thought might be helpful for others to read. When he offered the book to an advocate of one side of the issue, the person hurled the book against a wall without opening it. (I won't tell you which side of the debate the book hurler was on, but you probably guessed wrong.)

I expect that, in time, cooler heads will prevail and we will eventually wonder what all the fuss was about. For now, however, the matter inspires a great deal of sound and fury.

International relations

Because our church has been an immigrant church, we Lutherans have relatives living on every part of the globe. We often have first-hand information about what is happening in the daily lives of the people in the places that make the news.

The ELCIC is a member in the Lutheran World Federation and the World Council of Churches. This helps us to learn about what is going on in the world. These partnerships also help us to take part in efforts to make this world a better place.

The ELCIC is also an active partner in a number of Canadian inter-church social justice coalitions. These coalitions are uniquely Canadian and provide the ELCIC with research and resources that would not otherwise be available to it. For example, the ecumenical initiatives of Canadian churches are part of the international pressure that is causing change in South Africa.

When it was organized in 1986, one of the first actions taken by the ELCIC was to "publicly and un-equivocally reject existing apartheid systems." Member churches of the Lutheran World Federation felt so strongly about the matter that they suspended the membership of two white South African churches until they were willing to take a similar stand.

Through Canadian Lutheran World Relief, we are involved in many development and relief efforts in a number of "Third World" countries. Long before the world press focused on Somalia, Lutherans had been flying aid into that country. We do not try to operate on our own but cooperate with many other international development and service agencies as well as with Canadian government initiatives.

Our experiences have been teaching us that important changes must be made to the world's economic and social order for any real change in the living conditions of the so-called developing nations to happen. We must learn to live together or together we will destroy our planet.

Militarism

In the past, most Lutherans followed what is called the "just war theory." This says that war is always sinful and evil, but there are times when Christians have to take part in war. Martin Luther saw defense, particularly defense of our neighbors, as the only reason that Christians should take part in a war.

This position still has strong support among Lutherans. However, we also face the insanity of nuclear arsenals and the vast amounts of money being spent on weapons. This money could instead be used to take care of the health, education, and well-being of the people the military claims to protect. This has been causing Lutherans to rethink their position. A small but increasingly vocal minority is saying that the Christian tradition of pacifism would be more appropriate.

Racism

Lutherans believe that every person is created in God's image. That means that each person is special and that the community has an obligation to protect each person's human rights and each person's participation in the community.

In a 1964 statement, Lutherans said, "Injurious discrimination based on race is a violation of God's created order, of the redemption of Christ, and of the nature of the Church." Most of us believe that racism is wrong. For many of us the matter was theoretical. Few people with differently colored skin lived in our communities or attended our churches.

Then Canadian immigration patterns began to change. The faces in some of our congregations have begun to reflect this change, but most of our congregations in Canada are still very Caucasian. We have to do some serious thinking about the extent to which racism plays a part in who does or doesn't join us at worship.

In a survey conducted at the beginning of the '90s, Lutheran youth identified racism as one of the biggest problems facing Canadian society. The riots, on both sides of the border, that followed the "not guilty" verdict of the police who beat Rodney King proved that our youth are more in tune with reality than the rest of us.

The congregation that I served in North York, Ontario, was racially and ethnically diverse. We had some very interesting pot-luck meals. Not only were we enriched by new culinary delights, we enriched each other's lives as we shared the stories of our faith.

Sex

The ELCIC advocates that sexual relationships take place in the context of a lifelong relationship between two loving partners who have made a public commitment of fidelity to each other.

Some of our members will say that that doesn't go far enough. Others will say that those are just fancy words that avoid a clear stand. Still others will get upset by what they think might be implied by what is not said in those words.

And still others will say, "What's all the fuss about? I don't care what you say. People will be people. No matter what we say, you won't stop them from having sex."

Lutherans don't want to stop people from having sex. We do want people to be loving and responsible sexual beings.

Sexism

There are still those in our church who do not want to admit that sexism is a problem. They claim that the problem is only in the minds of a few "radical women's libbers." Too many still deny the inequality and injustice that exists because of gender discrimination.

Unfortunately, the problem is not in the minds of a

128

few, but in the mind-set of far too many of our members. The church is slowly catching up to the changing roles of women and men in church and society. The ways we use language and the choices we make in electing or selecting our leadership tell the story of a church struggling to overcome sexism.

The ELCIC Consulting Committee on Women and Men is trying to work at the problem. However, at some of the synod conventions held in 1992, female clergy still reported that they were not considered for calls simply because they were women. One synod convention's nominating committee was chastised for bringing in a slate of nominees for election that was almost exclusively male.

Sexual abuse

Several women have recently pressed charges against male clergy for sexual abuse. Much of the church reacted with shock and disbelief. Many people moved to protect and support the abusers. Some offered support for the abused.

The ELCIC was literally caught with its pants down and is now struggling to clean up its act. This means that policies and procedures are being developed which are intended to do more than look good in print. The church is recognizing that abuse cannot be tolerated.

The ELCIC has said that abuse of any sort is wrong. It has begun to educate itself and others about the realities of abuse. Very early in its existence, it provided a resource focusing on spousal abuse called "Broken Promises." Steps have been taken to train pastors and lay people to deal with abuse of all sorts. Policies have recently been set in place to provide official guidance for the church to deal with abuse on an official level.

Churchgoer values

Several studies, particularly by Reginald Bibby of the University of Lethbridge, have found that no matter what churches teach, the opinions of Canadians who go to church aren't much different from those of other

Canadians. Sadly, Lutherans can be lumped right in there with the rest of those who ignore the church's guidance.

However, another study by the Gallup research organization found that people who are deeply involved in the life of their churches and synagogues **do** tend to pay attention to what is being taught. Gallup found that these people are three times more active than others in social, charitable, and civic activities such as feeding the hungry, housing the homeless, and caring for the sick.

To soar like eagles

It's hard to soar with the eagles when you hang around with a bunch of turkeys. Sometimes we waste so much energy debating whether or not something is too left-wing or too right-wing that the thing never gets off the ground.

Even when we do reach an agreement, after the vote is taken and the decision is put in print, most people, even those in the ELCIC, aren't aware that we have said anything. Sometimes, when people eventually do find out what was decided, they still say, "What a bunch of turkeys!"

So why do we bother trying? Because every now and then, we get off the ground and we make a significant difference.

The prophet Isaiah wrote these words of hope for people who were afraid that injustice would never end: "...those who wait for the LORD shall renew their strength, they shall mount up with wings like eagles." (Isaiah 40:31)

Chapter 9

Bishop Telmor Sartison

Pastors, preachers, and other creatures

Since I'm one of those people who sometimes puts a collar on backwards and climbs into the pulpit to preach, you might think that I have the inside track on ministry in this ELCIC of ours. Well, yes and no. You see, we are still sorting out how we do things in this new church, and one of the things that we are sorting out is how we do ministry.

In the first place, ministry is something that we **all** do. Ministry is **our** ministry because we were baptized.

"All Christians are set apart by Baptism to carry out their calling to a lifelong ministry in the world. This ministry of the baptized is fundamental to all ministries in Christ's church." This is the way ministry in the ELCIC was explained in one ELCIC report.

131

However, there are specialized kinds of ministry as well. If you are a lay person, you have a ministry, a calling, that is uniquely **yours**, and I, as a member of the clergy, have a ministry, a calling, that is uniquely **mine**. Sometimes we have difficulty sorting out what is yours, mine, and ours because the lines between the various ministries are blurred.

Sorting it out

What I've just said is fine, but you and I know that most people don't talk about the things that lay people do as ministry, even if they are done in the name of Jesus. A layperson might do ministry, but no one is going to stick a "Rev" in front of that person's name.

Most people would say that a "minister" is an ordained person. The work this person does is "ministry."

So in this chapter that's the way I'll talk too. I've already talked about the ministry that is ours and the ministry that is specially yours in the chapter called "What we do with what we've got." I've also given you some idea of the roles laypeople play in the chapter "What happens the rest of the week."

The good, the bad, and the so-so

When I was in seminary, the office secretary confided that, before she came to work at the seminary, she had this idea that pastors even wore those backward collars when they went to bed. As she got to know a whole lot of pastors and people who wanted to be pastors, she learned that we are people just like everyone else.

We have high standards to live up to. Those standards should apply just as much to everyone else. Just because you may not be a pastor doesn't mean that God expects any less of you than me. Every one of God's people is important, and what every one of us does is equally important.

Being a pastor does not give anyone the inside track with God. We are not any "holier than thou." Unfortunately there are a few pastors who believe that God made some of us a little more equal than others. There are also a few laypeople who let such pastors get away with that kind of thinking.

Most of the clergy that I know are sincere, decent, caring people who try very hard to live what they preach and teach. I think it is important to say that at a time when we hear so many reports about clergy who have gone bad.

There are pastors who take advantage of the power of their position and who use it to abuse the very people they are called to help and serve. There are also ministers who bungle things so badly that you wonder how they ever got past the examining committee. The bunglers are annoying, but the abusive pastors are terrifying.

Being a pastor doesn't guarantee success, or a happy marriage, or kids who turn out to be their parents' pride and joy. We pastors often make a miserable mess of things. However, most of us have a strong faith, and we draw on the resources of the Christian community to see us through the good times and the bad. But you don't have to be ordained for that, right?

Ordained

People sometimes wonder how I got to be a pastor. I sometimes wonder about that myself.

I had admired some of the pastors whom I had seen, and people said they thought I had the makings of a pastor. I had dropped out of high school and was attending business college and driving truck when Pastor Vernon Cronmiller gave me a ride home from a meeting. "Just what do you think you're doing with your life?" Vern asked.

"Why don't you mind your own —— business," I snapped as I slammed the car door and stomped away. But he got me thinking. I found that I felt compelled to be a pastor. I completed high school, college, seminary, and was ordained.

But it doesn't matter how much a person feels that God wants them to be a pastor, the church has to agree that it also wants you to be a pastor.

There is a long period of sorting things through. It's not just a matter of three years of study at a seminary. The preparation involves special training programs in parishes and other places such as hospitals and prisons. Normally a person serves in a ministry situation for at least a year under the supervision of a pastor before that person is approved for ordination. There is also psychological screening and interviews by an examining committee. Finally the church agrees that you may be ordained.

What I've just described is the normal process to become an ordained minister in the ELCIC. There are several exceptions to the norm, but I won't try to confuse you with all those.

Technically, no one except an ordained pastor may preach or administer the sacraments. Exceptions are sometimes allowed to that rule, and it may be broken for baptism in an emergency. Sometimes a layperson is licensed by a bishop to administer Communion when a pastor is not available.

Ordination is not just a matter of ability or training. Some laypeople may be better trained in theology than their pastor. Some might be better public speakers. But we select certain people whom we believe are specially gifted by God. We call them pastors and ask them to devote themselves to this ministry.

We try to avoid letting other people onto the pastor's turf. This is not because the pastor is necessarily a special person (although we trust she or he is) but because this ministry is special. We want to make sure that we have done our best to see that it is done properly and not on the basis of someone's peculiar whim.

Diaconal ministers and other pastors

Now to complicate things. In some congregations you will find a person called a diaconal minister. These people might preach on occasion, but they are specialists in areas such as education, music, or administration. They are not permitted to administer the Sacraments. That is reserved exclusively for pastors.

Some people in the ELCIC feel that we should ordain diaconal ministers. Others want to recognize their special gifts but don't think that ordination is the way to do this. The ELCIC is still working out the details on diaconal ministry. From what I've seen in other denominations with similar practices, it can become very confusing since there are laypeople who do similar work without being ordained.

To complicate things further, many ordained ministers don't work in parishes. Some of that makes sense. There are chaplains in hospitals, prisons, campuses, and the military who do many of the things people normally associate with pastors.

Then there are people like me who seldom stand in a pulpit. I'm a magazine editor because that's the way the ELCIC has called me to minister.

A number of us pastors serve as administrators in the national office in Winnipeg, and through the synod offices as well as in a number of other church institutions. Some may serve overseas with the Lutheran World Federation or with the World Council of Churches. Some may be missionaries. There is also another group of us who work as professors at seminaries and colleges, and who teach at high school. Many of the people I've just mentioned serve alongside laypeople who serve in the same way.

Rostered

Sometimes what we do isn't very much different from what a whole lot of other people who don't have "Rev" stuck on the front of their names do. So why us and not the rest?

Well, we are "rostered," that is, we are on an official list that says that we are clergy of the ELCIC. That means that the ELCIC takes official (and legal) responsibility for our actions.

It also means that we are formally held accountable to the ELCIC for our ministry. For example, I have to write a report about my ministry each year for my bishop.

Sounds like serious stuff, doesn't it? Just think how much could be done if everyone took their ministry as seriously.

Being a bishop

I've mentioned another group of ministers called bishops. We are still thinking about the possibility of a special ordination for bishops. There are six of these people in the ELCIC. One leads the entire ELCIC, while the other five lead the five synods.

At one time their position in the church was called "president." These people acted a bit like the chief executive officer of the church or the synod. Over time, people began to feel that the church is not a business corporation and should identify its leaders with a title more fitting to a church leader.

They also began to feel that there should be more emphasis on the pastoral role of these people as op-posed to the "business executive" role.

While we've identified the ministry of the bishops as unique, we still haven't worked out exactly what we expect them to do. You will find them presiding at special events in the life of the church. They often chair conventions and have legal responsibilities as chief executive officers. They become especially important to a congregation that is looking for a minister because the congregation is supposed to work with the bishop to find a minister.

The national bishop is elected by a convention of the ELCIC, and the synodical bishops by their particular synod, to a four-year term. Suppose the members of the ELCIC or of the synod don't like the way the bishop has acted, or perhaps they feel a change is needed. In such cases, a new bishop may be elected when the present bishop's term ends.

Some people think of the bishops as the bosses. My experience with bishops is that "boss" is the last word they would pick to talk about themselves. They would probably describe themselves as the chief servants of the church.

Lutheran ministers and congregations insist on a great deal of freedom, and bishops seldom interfere with that freedom unless there is a serious problem which cannot be solved in any other way. Most of the time bishops have to get by on the power of persuasion and the good will of the people to get things done.

Other church staff

I know that I said that this chapter would be about the people that we usually call ministers, but there is a group of special people who are not ordained but whose ministries must not be overlooked. These people may be volunteers, or they may receive wages for their part-time or full-time service.

One of them is the congregational secretary. A good church secretary knows everyone, knows where everything is kept, remembers who gave or did what and when, and can say why we do or don't do things that way around here.

A parish which lets its pastor play secretary is making poor use of the pastor's talents. Even if the pastor knows how to type and can run the printer, do you really want the pastor running off the Sunday bulletin instead of polishing Sunday's sermon or visiting in the parish?

Caretakers are also important people. There is something extra special about a church which is well-taken care of. Well scrubbed and polished floors, sparkling windows, well-groomed lawns and trim flower beds, walks cleared of snow—each thing sends a silent signal that this place is worth putting some time into.

Then there is the organist or music director (some congregations have both). Very few congregations can afford a full-time person, and some rely on volunteers. These people are key to worship.

Even though some congregations find that they are forced to accept anyone who can play a few notes on a piano, selecting a church musician with proper training is nearly as important as finding a pastor. These people hold the service together. Their music sets the tone and

137

the mood of worship.

Blessed is the congregation which has a secretary, caretaker, or musician who understands that theirs is an important ministry and not merely a job to be done as quickly as possible.

A day in the life of a pastor

I wanted to describe a typical day in the life of a pastor, but there is no such thing. The pastor might plan to do some office work in the morning, some hospital or home visiting in the afternoon, and to attend at least one meeting in the evening.

But then the telephone rings, and it rings, and it rings again: "Can I come over and see you right away? I need to talk to someone." "We've just rushed George to the hospital. He's had a heart attack." "Sue and I want to get married this spring. What arrangements do we need to make with you?" "Pastor, this is Tom over at the funeral home. We have a family here who say that they are Lutheran but they haven't been to any church for quite a while and I was wondering if you could help them out." "Billy's got the measles. I know that you were counting on him to help you, but I'm afraid you'll have to find someone else this week." "I know that this is supposed to be your day off... I hope I haven't interrupted your supper... I know it's late/ early/ but ..."

Even when the phone isn't ringing

I'm writing this section to give you a picture of what the pastor may do behind the scenes in an attempt to help you do your ministry. Perhaps these glimpses may help all of us serve together better.

What does or does not happen in a congregation is not an accident. Things happen because someone planned or failed to plan for them. Many times that planner is the pastor—sometimes working with the help and support of many others in the parish, sometimes with very little help or support.

All organizations have a lot of paperwork that must be done and congregations are no exception. Some pastors delight in administration. Others see it as a necessary evil.

Occasionally, a pastor is blessed with members who wonder why the pastor should be pushing paper, and so they help with the administrative details. Some larger parishes hire a professional administrator to free the pastor for pastoring.

Then there are meetings and more meetings. Each one takes prior planning. There are classes to teach and study groups to lead. And still more time needed for preparation.

Some pastors also serve as a kind of volunteer coordinator since most people who serve in the church are volunteers. They recruit teachers, committee members, worship leaders, and often provide a lot of training and guidance for these people as well.

Working with volunteers demands incredible tact and patience. Some people don't do what they say they will. Others can't do what they think they can. Some need someone to hold their hand almost every step of the way, while others need a firm hand to keep them in check.

More than one pastor has cried in despair, "Whoever said this was 'organized' religion?" It has also convinced many that we live by the grace of God.

The sermon

How does a pastor write and preach a sermon week after week after week? It's about ten percent inspiration and 90 percent perspiration, and the closer Sunday gets the more you sweat.

Ideally, I think that a pastor should spend at least one hour preparing and writing for every minute spent in the pulpit. Sometimes that actually happens, if the phone doesn't ring and you can find a bit of time between all the other demands for your attention.

Pastoral conversations

One of the most important parts of pastoring is being available for people. Pastors never know when or where someone will need them. It can start with a simple "Hi! How's it going?" while picking up some groceries, and end in a long answer that deserves a sympathetic ear, even if the ice cream is beginning to melt.

The better the pastor listens, the more people begin to share their joys, fears, hopes, sorrows, and challenges. Those friendly chats can do a world of good for many.

However, let the chatterers beware. There is a growing trend to think of pastors as counselors. Some pastors are very well trained and could hang up their shingle as a professional counselor even if they weren't a pastor. Others have only a smattering of classroom theory and perhaps a few hours of supervised training. That's why I prefer to use the term pastoral conversation rather than counseling.

Wise pastors know when they don't have the time or the training to give the proper help. They will refer the person to a doctor or counselor who can do the job. That doesn't mean they don't care. It means that they care enough to see that the person gets the very best.

Community ministry

I firmly believe that a congregation must minister beyond the four walls of its building and to more than the people who claim membership. Since clergy are often the people the community most readily recognize as being from a particular congregation, many clergy are also very active in community service.

When I was a parish pastor, I found that I could do a lot of good, both for the parish and the community, by serving on various boards and committees connected with health care services and education. Others get involved in the political process. A few of our clergy are municipal council members, school board trustees, mayors and parliamentarians.

It is a good way to meet people, and a pastor who serves well in the community gives a positive witness to the church. It also keeps clergy in touch with what is going on in people's lives.

Most communities have an organization for clergy from all denominations. Some of these play a leading role in the life of the community. Others are little more than an excuse for a group of pastors to get together over coffee and chat.

I found that my participation with pastors from other denominations was always worthwhile, both for myself and for my parish. I learned about community resources and who to contact for what. Sometimes an exciting project or program turned up that put some extra zip in the life of all our parishes. I can't begin to measure the value of the numerous friendships I made from those monthly meetings.

Clergy need time to get together with each other to talk shop, to grumble about problems, to learn and pray and play together. Pastors are under incredible stress and many burn out because they don't get the care and support they need.

Clergy and the whole church

Some clergy pay very little attention to the church beyond their congregation. Others find the extra time spent on wider church projects very rewarding.

Some members do not realize that clergy on the ELCIC roster have certain responsibilities beyond their parish. Clergy are expected to take part in conference and synod meetings and to serve on various committees of the church and synod when they are elected or called upon. Congregations are expected to put money in the budget to help make this happen.

This can lead to tension in a parish. Some congregational members identify what the pastor does beyond the parish as volunteer work that cuts into the time that should be spent on parish work. They don't realize that this "outside" work is a legitimate part of a pastor's overall responsibilities. The conference or synod or ELCIC is not "them;" it is "us."

However, there are times when a pastor **does** get so involved in the work of the larger church, that he or she seems to forget the work that still needs to be done back home. Sometimes, if the congregational members are not as tactful as they might be, or if the pastor is

141

not as mature as one would like, this leads to confrontation and conflict. Having a sense of humor helps. One congregation helped their overactive pastor gain perspective by "reissuing" him his call.

Occupational hazards

Most clergy are overachievers. They want everything in the parish to run smoothly. They are often very talented people who can do many things well. So they start to do things that other people should be doing, just to get them done.

When I served in the parish, I wasn't very good at keeping my fingers out of other people's areas of responsibility. I wish that I had read and heeded the advice Ralph Milton gives in his book *This United Church of Ours*. His wife is a minister. So he knows of what he speaks. Much of this book parallels his, but it uses my words and experiences. This time I need to let Ralph have his say. I'll sit back and listen and hope a few of you do the same:

It's the people of the congregation who are responsible for the life and work of the church. The minister is their resource person. It's not the other way around.

The minister ought to know, generally, what's going on. At least about the main activities. But it's a healthy thing for clergy to be quite clueless about who is locking up after the meeting or whether the phone bill got paid last month. Clergy should work hard at not knowing how to fix anything around the church. They should never know where anybody put anything. (*This United Church of Ours, pg. 104*)

A pastor explained it this way. At a church council meeting, one of the members was spouting off about a certain passage of scripture with very badly mangled theology. The pastor corrected him, and the member began to object. "Look," said the pastor. "I attended seminary for four years and have done a lot of studying of the Bible and theology over the years

142

as well. Do you have that kind of training, Bob?"

"No," admitted Bob.

"Well, then let me do what I am here for and listen to what I have to say," replied the pastor.

Later in the meeting, the council was dealing with a financial problem. The pastor began to argue vigorously about the way it was being tackled when suddenly he caught himself and turned to Bob.

"Bob," he said, "you're a businessman with a lot of experience in dealing with finances, aren't you?"

"Well, yes I am," said Bob.

"Now it's my turn to let you do what you are here for and for me to shut up and listen," said the pastor.

The paradoxes of being a pastor

During the time that I served as a parish pastor, I found that life was filled with contradictions which sometimes threatened to drive me around the bend.

The people who expected me to be a regular visitor often complained the loudest when I wasn't in the office. They were also the ones who were seldom home when I called. Trying to set a time to drop by sometimes meant running a gauntlet of conflicting dates and other delaying tactics.

Hospital visiting was a special problem. In a big city with many hospitals, there is no way to drop by and see who's there. More and more hospitals don't even list patients by religious group any more. Yet there are those who get very indignant because "the pastor didn't visit me when I was in hospital," even though they never told anyone that they were in hospital until they were back on their feet and back in church.

The care and feeding of our clergy

Like many other very dedicated people, clergy often don't know when to quit or how to say no. Too many pastors work 80-hour weeks and feel guilty about the other things they meant to do but never got around to.

Our clergy suffer for that and so do their families. More than one pastor's spouse has complained, "I

143

married you, not your job." Life in a clergy family is no different from life in any other family where mom or dad has a very active and demanding career. It can go just as sour if the family members don't make time to be a family.

The hours that a minister puts in are often very long. The demands can become so great that pastors forget to take time off for themselves and their families. My wife once lined up our two children at the door as I was leaving for yet another meeting. "Children, this is your father," she said. "Kenn, this is your daughter, Teri-Lyn, and your son, Jeffrey." I got the message.

My family noticed two significant changes when I left parish ministry. They thought it was great to have a pastor who was not their husband or their dad. They also like that I have more time for them. Often it's just the simple fact that I'm around the house puttering at something instead of off to another meeting.

Congregations can help clergy gain perspective and learn how to say no. Sometimes they have to get very tough with pastors who are busy driving themselves to burnout.

Before a pastor accepts a call, the parish agrees to certain working conditions. These conditions are necessary if we are to have healthy and whole people in our pulpits and the other places where we want ministry to happen.

Clergy are supposed to take at least four weeks vacation. There are extra weeks built into some agreements after certain periods of service and for certain levels of experience and responsibility.

Clergy should have at least one day a week all to themselves. But there are many weeks when that never happens because of sudden funerals or other pastoral emergencies.

That's why it is unfair to ask a pastor to return from vacation to conduct a funeral. Not returning from vacation for a funeral doesn't mean that the pastor doesn't care. It means that, if the **pastor** isn't cared for, he or she won't be able to care for others very long or very effectively. Sometimes that vacation is the only extended chunk of free time that person has had for many hectic months.

Certainly your family is going through a traumatic time, and you would appreciate the pastor being there. But think of the pastor's family who also find it very traumatic never to have that person fully part of their family, except on vacation.

Contracts with clergy also spell out time for study leave each year. That's not a neat perk that gives clergy a chance to goof off, although goofing off is sometimes exactly what is needed. Ministry is very complex and demanding. Every year there are all sorts of chances for clergy to learn things that will help them and the people they were called to serve.

If you aren't aware of your pastor taking time for study leave, ask him or her what they are doing with their study time. If the answer is a shrug and a mumbled excuse about not having enough time, push the issue. Clergy never know everything they need to know.

Ralph Milton says, "Burnout and rustout are occupational hazards for clergy. Holidays help the burnout. Study leave helps the rustout." (*This United Church of Ours, pg. 105*)

Coming and going

Some people think that the minister is the boss of the congregation, or maybe the head of the congregation. In fact, the elected chairperson of the congregational council is its chief executive officer. In a sense, every member of the congregation is kind of a boss; every member has a say in how that congregation ministers.

This doesn't mean that the minister is a mere employee who can be told what to do, when and where. The relationship is really more like a marriage. One or the other of the spouses isn't the boss. They are partners. A pastor and a parish are partners in ministry. As partners, they try to help and encourage each other to minister as effectively as they can.

Just as marriages can break down and end in divorce, there are also times when the bond between pastor and parish break down. The congregation cannot fire the pastor. Technically, if the pastor doesn't commit heresy or do something so gross that everyone agrees that person should not be a pastor any more, the pastor can remain in the parish until he or she decides to leave or retire.

There is an exception to this arrangement that is becoming more common. Sometimes a pastor doesn't want to make a long time commitment to a parish. Or maybe the parish wants to try a particular direction in ministry, but isn't sure how it will work out, or if there will really be enough money to keep it going for more than a limited time. In such cases, the pastor and the parish agree to a "term call" which has a fixed date when the pastor will leave or, in most cases, when the agreement can be renewed if everything is working out well.

I was in a situation once where I was the regular pastor of one congregation while serving another under a term call. Neither congregation had the resources nor the need for a full-time pastorate. We all made sure that the arrangements were clearly understood. We also had a set time each year to meet together to make sure that both congregations and I were still satisfied with the arrangement. Eventually we parted ways by mutual agreement and with the feeling that all of us had been enriched by sharing ministry together.

For really serious problems with a pastor, there is a messy and complicated process in which the bishop of the synod forms a committee to investigate specific charges. Fortunately things seldom get to that point.

Calling a pastor

We don't talk about hiring ministers; we call them. This "call" has some very deliberate stages.

The calling of a pastor provides a wonderful opportunity for congregations to really learn what it means to be part of the ELCIC. People can't just go out and ask anyone they like to be the minister of their congregation.

The congregation has to work with the bishop, and

they can only call people who are properly approved to be a minister by the ELCIC through one of its synods. In some cases the search goes far beyond Canada, especially when a special language skill is needed. There is also a fairly free and easy exchange of clergy between the ELCIC and its sister church in the United States, the Evangelical Lutheran Church in America.

Different bishops and different congregations prefer different ways of matching the right pastor with the right parish. When things finally reach the stage where the congregation has decided that a certain person should be its minister, the congregation takes a vote and then issues a "call."

This call is a written document that explains the basic things expected of the minister and of the congregation. Many of these are standard expectations that apply to any pastor in the ELCIC; sometimes a special task or two is added to suit a local situation. Most people don't give much thought to these things except when they are calling a pastor or setting the annual budget. Naturally pastors are more knowledgeable about the terms of the call since those terms directly affect the pastor's responsibilities and livelihood.

Congregations are sometimes surprised to find that they must meet a list of conditions: housing, salary level, pension, vacation time allowed and so on. These conditions aren't dreamed up by the pastor. They are standards which are set by the synod in convention. Representatives from every congregation have voted on them. Congregations can go beyond the basic expectations but they are not supposed to offer anything less.

It is unusual for a Lutheran congregation to consider anyone other than a Lutheran pastor. However, in some isolated situations, special agreements are made with clergy from other denominations.

In some communities, several denominations will combine their resources and be served by a pastor from one of the denominations. This is called shared ministry. This arrangement is commonly entered into between members of the ELCIC, the Anglican Church, the

Presbyterian Church and the United Church.

Time for a change
There are no rules for how long a minister should stay in a parish. Sometimes they never leave. Sometimes it only **feels** like they will never leave.

There are many reasons why a pastor might move. Sometimes the person just goes stale. Both the pastor and the people need something fresh. Or someone in the minister's family has needs, such as a health problem or schooling, which involve moving the whole family.

It is not unusual for a new minister to stay in his or her first parish for about three years before moving on—perhaps because that's how long it sometimes takes for a parish to smooth off a rookie's rough edges. Sadly, it can also be that the parish doesn't want to pay the money that more experience deserves. In a few cases, the parish simply doesn't have the money. Regrettably, some clergy also play a bigger-is-better game. Fortunately such parishes and clergy are in the minority.

Interim ministry
Sometimes a parish has a tough time getting its act together. Maybe the last pastor left after a terrific fight that almost split the parish. Or maybe a loved and respected pastor retired after a long and fruitful ministry. Perhaps the parish doesn't have any clear sense of where it wants to go with future ministry.

For whatever reason, the parish needs to work through many emotions and issues before it is ready for a long-term relationship with another pastor. Sometimes a pastor will agree to serve the congregation for a limited time with the intent of helping the congregation to sort itself out and to make specific plans for the future.

While any pastor may be called on to do this, more and more pastors who serve this way have received special training as interim ministers. Their work may take a few months, or even a year or two. They use a variety of techniques to help the parish get back on track. Their greatest satisfaction comes when a new pastor can begin ministry in a renewed congregation.

All shapes and sizes

Ministers in the ELCIC come from many different places around the world. They are a multilingual and multiracial lot, even though a significant number are English-speaking Canadian-born Caucasians.

When I entered seminary in 1969, there were no female pastors in Lutheran churches in Canada. One of my classmates, Anna Mazak, was the first woman to attend our seminary with the goal of ordination. We males with our big egos thought that she was looking for a husband until she presented her first paper. Then we had to scramble to keep up with her.

North American Lutherans began to ordain women in 1970. On May 7, 1976, another classmate, Pamela McGee, became the first woman in Canada to be ordained as a Lutheran pastor. Over the years, she has been joined by many other women. Some seminary classes now have more women than men.

I wish I could report that female pastors have the same opportunities as male pastors in the ELCIC. It's starting to happen, but just starting. A couple of our larger parishes have called women clergy as senior pastors instead of as assistant pastors. But many congregations still won't consider a woman, and the hierarchy of the ELCIC remains pretty much a male domain.

When Donald W. Sjoberg retired as the first bishop of the ELCIC, a woman placed second in the balloting for a new bishop. This may be a sign that women are beginning to come into their own in the ELCIC, but I suspect that we will progress haltingly at best.

Another recent phenomenon is the emergence of clergy couples. People may not go to seminary looking for a spouse, but love has blossomed between some of our students. After marriage and graduation, what do you do with a couple who both want to serve as ministers?

Some parishes call both. Or two parishes near each other arrange calls so that the husband serves the one while the wife serves the other. As with every other case, the success of these ministries depends on the people involved.

Stereotypes

People sometimes ask me, "Are you sure that you're a minister?" At such times, I discover that I've shattered someone's myth about what ministers are like. Well, we don't come off some heavenly assembly line in a pastor factory.

Perhaps you imagine a cartoon character, a kindly, old, slightly out-of-it pastor sipping tea with the ladies. Yes, I am a tea-drinking parson. But I don't sip it from a cup, I drink it from a mug. And most of the "ladies" I've met in my ministry are very strong, intelligent women who blow the "church lady" image right out of the water.

For the record, I share the same feelings and face the same temptations that you do, as do the other people we call to be ministers. Unfortunately, ministers get saddled with many labels that have little or nothing to do with being a minister.

Sometimes pastors are accused of being "out of touch with what's really going on in the world." I have been called on to be pastor to murderers, thieves, adulterers, addicts, the abuser and the abused, the disturbed, the physically and mentally challenged, the sick and the dying, to name a few. There is little that you can tell me about people that would shock or surprise me. And I think I've had a pretty typical ministry.

Clergy spouses

At one time, it was normal for the pastor's spouse to think in terms of ministering to the needs of the parish along with the pastor. Some clergy spouses still see themselves as part of the pastoral team. But today such people are rare. A pastor's spouse is not part of a package deal. This can come as a bit of a shock to a congregation that was expecting two workers for the price of one when they called a married pastor.

When I was being interviewed by the call committee of one parish, they wanted to know what they could expect from my wife. I answered, "She expects to be treated like any other member. Don't ask her to help with something just because she happens to be married to the minister. Ask her because you need her help and the job suits her talents."

Quite often, today's clergy spouse has a career of his or her own. This can create quite a dilemma when considering a move. Sometimes a pastor will turn down a call because the spouse couldn't make the move without giving up a rewarding career. At other times a pastor resigns from a parish and becomes available for a call in another part of the country because the spouse's relocation means the pastor must move too.

Isolation and loneliness are often problems for clergy spouses; especially upon entering that first parish. Suddenly you find yourself in a community where no one knows you. To make matters worse, you are identified as a person you don't know—as the pastor's wife or the minister's husband.

My kids asked me to mention that life in the parsonage is no great picnic for pastors' kids either. Most "p.k.s" feel the strain of living life in a goldfish bowl. Pastors' kids often find it hard to live up to other people's unrealistic expectations. When you're a kid, you don't have much interest in being a "role model" for your peers. You want to do as they do.

A house to call home

Clergy families often face the difficulty of living in a house that they cannot really call their own. Fortunately, a growing number of congregations no longer provide a parsonage. Instead, they pay enough for the minister to rent or buy a place that suits the family's tastes, needs, and budget.

But many congregations still provide a "free" parsonage. Sometimes this is the only way a congregation can meet all its obligations to a pastor—the location or the cost of housing makes other alternatives impractical.

Living in a parsonage creates its own set of problems. Nothing can be changed or repaired or redecorated without permission, and what is done is often more in line with what the parish wants than what the family prefers. There is no chance to build up the equity that paying a mortgage gives. If a minister dies, the spouse has a few weeks to find another place to live. And when a minister retires the house they called home is suddenly no longer theirs.

Some formalities

Although I cover this in "Learning to speak Lutheran," it's probably good to repeat myself. We Lutherans usually call our ordained ministers "pastor." At least this holds true for those who have been ordained to a ministry of Word and Sacrament. The jury is still out on what name will be used for diaconal ministers.

So, if you are wondering what to call the minister, even if you can't remember the person's name, "pastor" is always acceptable. But you may also refer to or introduce us as you would most other people: "I would like you to meet Mary Johnson, our minister;" "I'm glad you could make it, Mr. Schmidt;" or "Hi, Pastor Kwok, how's it going?"

Many members of my parish called me "Pastor Kenn." Those who knew me really well simply called me "Kenn."

We prefer that you don't call one of our ministers "the reverend." We only use "Rev" when we put something down in writing.

Here's something else. Most people don't know that a backwards collar is not a required part of a pastor's dress code at any time. It's a useful symbol that a number of us use when we need people to be aware of our identity. But there is no law that stops anyone from putting on one of those collars.

Many of us are uncomfortable wearing that collar because it seems to make other people uncomfortable. Personally, I prefer to avoid the stereotypes by not wearing the collar and by letting the other person get to know me a bit first.

There is one piece of gear that is not optional for us and which no one but an ordained minister may wear. When we are in charge of the celebration of Holy Baptism or Holy Communion, we must wear our stole.

The stole is that piece of cloth that hangs around the minister's neck. It is a symbolic yoke that reminds us of Jesus' command to "Take my yoke upon you."

Anyone else can put on any of the other gear and that's okay. However, when you see someone wearing a stole, you know that this person has been trained and set aside by the church for the special duties of preaching the Word and of administering the Sacraments.

Hearing the call

Earlier in this chapter, I talked a bit about the training that we put our ministers through before we ordain them. We expect our ministers to be well trained. Normally we insist on an undergraduate degree as well as a theological degree. We also put the person through an internship. The person also has to be approved for ordination by an examining committee of a synod.

Just a few words for those who think that they might like to be ordained. The church can see that you have the formal education and it's not all that hard to answer the examining committee's questions to their satisfaction. But do you really have the makings of a minister?

One Sunday, my daughter, Teri-Lyn, read the lessons at one of our services. We had a number of visitors from a parish in the U.S. that morning. After the service, the wife of their pastor shook hands with Teri and complimented her on her reading. "You read very well, my dear," she said. "Tell me. Have you ever thought of being a minister like your father?"

"No way," Teri immediately replied.

"You are very wise, my dear," said the pastor's spouse. "We have eight children, and none of them have been foolish enough to follow in their father's footsteps."

Many of God's servants were reluctant to follow the call. Acting as an official spokesperson for God is an awesome responsibility. Moses and Jeremiah come to mind as examples. If you think that God might want you to be a minister, think again...and again, and again. It is very hard work. There are many rewards, but burnout and breakdown are common too.

Still, if you can't shake the idea, if something inside keeps pushing you in that direction and you find that you can't avoid the calling, then you can be fairly certain that the Holy Spirit is at work. If so, go ahead and God bless.

Age is not a factor. An increasing number of our pastors enter the ordained ministry after another career, or even several.

Some people feel a very strong and passionate call and they can't understand why they should go through all the training and other junk. If they are good enough for God, then why can't the church see that? Well, if you are the genuine article, a bit of time and church discipline never hurts.

It also helps to sort out most of the people who are on an emotional ego trip. They may think that they are sincere, but sincerely, I wouldn't want them for my pastor.

There are also a few people who enter seminary to find themselves. Seminary training may help you to learn many things. You may even learn a few things about yourself. However, if you don't find yourself before graduation, I hope you don't get ordained. There are enough lost people looking for hope and help in parishes without the parish having to nursemaid the pastor.

If you haven't been involved in a Lutheran congregation, I advise you to become a member of one for a couple of years before considering seminary. Most pastors spend the rest of their lives devoted to people and parishes just like the one in your neighborhood. Is that where you really want to spend most of your time?

Now a few words for those who have never thought of being ordained. Why not? God does amazing things with people just like you—sometimes ordination is one of those things. If God has that in mind for you, you're not going to shake it. Trust me. I know it from experience.

Homosexual clergy

The participation of homosexual persons in the life of the church has become an issue in most denominations, particularly if those persons feel called to be an ordained minister. The ELCIC accepts gays and lesbians as ordained ministers. We always have, and that surprises some people.

However, our practice is not to ordain a person who is a self-declared and practising homosexual. If such a person is already ordained and declares that he or she is a practising homosexual, that person will not be recommended for a call to a congregation by our bishops.

Our membership is divided in its opinions about homosexual pastors. Some of us consider homosexuality to be a curable condition that the Bible labels as sin. Others think it might be a natural, if different, way for some. These people are not convinced that the Bible speaks clearly about the matter.

It is an uncomfortable time for a single person to be a minister, no matter what that person's sexual orientation may be. Witch hunts and hysteria are not just part of the history of Salem, Massachusetts. Hopefully, we will deal with this as graciously as God deals with us. In the meantime, we need a lot more prayer and study before the Holy Spirit helps us to find our way.

A great bunch of people

As you've learned, we clergy in the ELCIC are a mixed bag of all sorts of people. Yes, there are a few rotten apples in the bunch, and a few of us are jerks. But when you really get to know us, you'll find that most of us are pretty terrific people.

We each have our particular strengths and our unique peculiarities, but the thing that most of us have in common is a genuine love of God and a strong love of people. That's why we put in long hours. It's why we get out of bed in the middle of the night to rush to a dying person's bedside, It's why we attend all those meetings, and preach, and teach, and visit. We care. We really do.

At one communion service, as I placed the bread

into the hands of the people kneeling there, I thought about all the lives I had the privilege of sharing Christ with at that moment: a couple struggling to keep their marriage alive, a woman who had tried to commit suicide, a troubled teen, a man just out of prison, a recovering alcoholic, a newlywed couple, a number of retired folk...

The benefit package on this job is fantastic!

Chapter 10

Martin Luther at the age of 50
Painting by Lucas Cranach the Elder, 1533

All in the family

Anyone who gets married knows that you don't just marry a person. You also join that person's family. When Diane and I got married, I knew that her relatives had shaped and influenced her life. I also knew that those people would now begin to have an influence on my life as well.

My mother-in-law (whom I affectionately call "Mrs. B") is a very important person in our lives. Her zest for life, her good sense, and her consideration for others have rubbed off not only on her daughter but also on the grandchildren Diane and I have given her. She's even managed to smooth off a few of my rough edges, either directly or through her daughter.

The ELCIC is part of a family too. The strongest

influence in our lives is our spiritual father—Martin Luther. Even though he died nearly 450 years ago, he still is very much alive in what we do and say.

There are also rifts in our Lutheran family that we have not been able to heal. A significant number of Lutherans in Canada belong to another denomination called the Lutheran Church—Canada. This division also influences us.

In this chapter I'll introduce you to Martin Luther as well as to the Lutheran Church—Canada.

Martin Luther's time

Martin Luther was born on November 10, 1483, in Eisleben, Germany. Fifteenth century Europe was about to emerge from the Middle Ages into the modern era. The world of Luther was a brutal world ruled by fear and plagued by superstition.

Government was a confusing mix of feudal states with a few free towns. Everyone was expected to know their place in the rigid order of things: peasants, priests, soldiers and nobility. Some areas were ruled by the church and others by princes. In many places it was hard to sort out the difference between the two.

The recently invented printing press began to open people's minds to new ideas. Columbus was about to make his way to the Americas. People worried about the threat of a Turkish invasion.

The structure of the Holy Roman Empire was beginning to crumble as people began to think of themselves as ethnic groups. The idea of nationhood was starting to grow. Small towns were becoming cities. A middle class interested in trade and commerce was emerging, and it wasn't interested in serving the interests of feudal lords. Peasants were beginning to question their lot in life.

Growing up

When Luther was about six months old, his parents, Hans and Margarethe Luther moved the family to nearby Mansfeld. His father was an ambitious man who managed to scrape enough money together to give his son an education.

Young Luther showed a great deal of promise. By 1502 he took his bachelor's degree and his master's in 1505. Then he began to study law.

One day Luther was caught in a violent storm. Lightning struck a nearby tree. Luther fell to the ground in terror. He prayed frantically to St. Anne, the special saint for miners (at one time his father had been a miner). He promised that if she would save his life, he would become a monk.

At the age of 22, in spite of his father's opposition, Luther entered a monastery in the Augustinian order.

Monk, priest, and scholar

Today we would advise Luther to lighten up and get a life. Like many others in his time, Luther was terrified of a God who wanted vengeance on sinners.

He was obsessed with trying to please God. He scrubbed floors and begged in the streets for money for the monastery. He read his Bible long into the night and confessed every sin he could think of, real and imagined. He even whipped himself.

Johann Staupitz, the head of Augustinian monasteries in Germany, was very concerned about the well-being of this young monk. Luther was ordained as a priest in 1507. Because of Luther's thirst for knowledge, Staupitz assigned him to teach at the new university in Wittenberg in 1508.

Luther still did not find peace. Staupitz sent him on an errand to Rome in 1510 hoping that the pilgrimage might have a settling influence. Instead, Luther was horrified at the extravagance and corruption of the Holy City.

Staupitz encouraged Luther to study for a doctor's degree, perhaps hoping to get Luther to think about other things. In 1512, Martin Luther became a doctor of sacred scripture and professor of Bible at Wittenberg University.

The turning point

Luther wondered how he could get God to accept

him. "How is one justified or made righteous?" was the way Luther asked it. The medieval church taught that a person had to earn God's acceptance.

As Luther studied and taught, he gradually began to realize that the New Testament teaches that grace cannot be earned. God gives grace. People do not make themselves acceptable to God. God freely accepts people. This became the doctrine of "justification by grace through faith."

Luther's discovery would soon challenge the entire church. The Roman Church taught that people needed the sacrament of penance to have their sins forgiven. To be forgiven, a person needed to confess to a priest and do good deeds to atone for their sins.

If the person had not done enough penance before dying, the unpaid debt had to be worked off in purgatory. Gradually, a system developed whereby a person could buy indulgences to offset punishment in purgatory. An indulgence is a document that says you are forgiven for doing something or other. Some were even bought before doing the deed! These indulgences began to be an important source of revenue for the church.

Pope Leo X needed money to complete the Church of St. Peter in Rome. He was willing to overlook a number of irregularities in the interest of raising the money he needed. One fundraiser was a Dominican prior, John Tetzel, who began to sell indulgences in a parish near to Luther's parish.

Some of Luther's parishioners bought indulgences from Tetzel. They challenged Luther when he questioned the way they were living by saying that Tetzel's indulgences had taken care of any sins they were committing.

On October 31, 1515, Luther tacked up a notice on the door of the Castle Church. It was an invitation to the theologians of Wittenberg to meet with Luther and to debate the indulgence situation. Luther put down his ideas on the notice in 95 points or 95 theses. As Luther tacked up his notice, the sound of his hammer echoed in Rome.

Confrontation

To Luther's surprise, his 95 theses were reprinted. Within two weeks they were being discussed all over Germany. A copy soon reached Rome. The Pope apparently brushed the matter off as a minor row. The Dominicans charged Luther with heresy. He was ordered to appear in Rome to stand trial.

Frederick the Wise, elector of Saxony, governed the territory where Luther lived. After some political wrangling, Frederick insisted that Luther be tried on German soil.

Attempts at diplomacy failed when John Ek and Luther entered into a debate at Leipzig University. Luther forcefully stated his case and directly challenged the authority of the Pope. After that Luther began to write several books which criticized the Pope's power.

At the heart of Luther's arguments was his conviction that grace is a gift of God which sets people free. This freedom made each person "subject to none." It also set people free from looking inward and worrying about God's approval. This energized them to use their freedom to serve their neighbors out of love.

From priest to outlaw

On June 15, 1520, Pope Leo signed a papal bull. This document charged Luther with heresy and gave him 60 days to appear for trial. Anyone who protected him would be excommunicated. Luther's books were to be burned.

However, Luther had become a popular hero in Germany. On December 10, at the end of the 60-day period, Luther stepped up to a bonfire outside the gates of Wittenberg and quietly put the papal bull in the fire. In Rome's eyes he had become an outlaw.

Meanwhile, the Holy Roman Empire had a new emperor, Charles V, whose father was German. When he was crowned as emperor, Charles had made a constitutional change that said no German could be taken outside the country for trial, and that no one should be outlawed without a hearing.

Bound by conscience

Charles V convened an imperial assembly (called a "diet") at Worms, Germany, to deal with state business. Charles offered Luther safe conduct to Worms for a hearing.

Large crowds turned out to cheer Luther along the way. Cities welcomed him and invited him to preach. The streets of Worms were so jammed with people that Luther could barely get through.

When he appeared before the Diet, Luther was asked two questions: "Did he write the books which were standing on a table? Was he willing to recant what he had written?" Luther asked for some time to think over his answer.

The following afternoon, when Luther began to give an explanation of his material, he was told to give a direct answer to the question of whether or not he would recant.

Luther's famous reply: "Unless convinced by the testimony of Scripture or right reason—for I trust neither the Pope nor councils inasmuch as they have often erred and contradicted one another—I am bound by conscience, held captive by the Word of God in the Scriptures I have quoted. I neither can nor will recant anything, for it is neither right nor safe to act against conscience. God help me! Amen."

"George the knight"

Because he was still under the promise of safe conduct, Luther set out again for Wittenberg. While on the road he was "kidnapped." Soon after that a bearded knight, Junker George, was seen at Wartburg, an ancient fortress-castle near Eisenach. Frederick the Wise had found a way to protect his subject who was now an outlaw in both the eyes of the church and the empire.

While at Wartburg, Luther translated the New Testament into German, the language of his people. He continued to be an important influence in Germany, and his writings were widely read.

Meanwhile, extremists destroyed organs, paintings,

and statues. They attacked priests and worshipers who tried to continue with their traditions. Luther returned to Wittenberg and restored order. He insisted that no changes would be made until people had time to think things over and to decide what changes were appropriate for them.

The emperor, Charles V, became too distracted by problems with France and with the Turks to pay much attention to Luther. So Luther was free to preach and write and teach at Wittenberg.

Luther's legacy

Luther was a very cautious and conservative reformer. While he said many things that are worth holding on to, some of what he said is unacceptable to modern Lutherans. (After all, Luther was as much of a saint as he was a sinner—just like the rest of us.)

For example, after World War II, Luther scholars were appalled and ashamed to discover that Nazi Germany had found support in Luther's anti-Semitic writings.

Luther had taught about freedom. However, when the peasants revolted and demanded social reform, Luther preached the Christian duty of submission to authority. He wrote an article that condemned their revolt and gave permission to the authorities to slaughter any peasant who opposed them.

Luther himself was very conscious of being both a great sinner and a great saint. He would agree with attempts to make an honest and complete evaluation of who he was, even though such attempts might offend some who call themselves Lutherans.

As a former monk, Luther understood the monastic system. Now he worked against that system of which he had been such an enthusiastic part. On June 13, 1525, the ex-monk married a former nun named Katherina von Bora. They had six children and became role models for Lutheran clergy families.

Katie was good for Luther. She probably extended his life by bringing order and stability to it with her efficient housekeeping and thrifty management of their finances. Their home was known for its music and many guests.

A new German church began to emerge. Luther encouraged congregations to take responsibility for themselves, to choose pastors and provide for the education of the people. He wrote the Small Catechism so that people would have a simple way of learning and teaching the basics of the faith. He revised worship. He put it into the language of the people and wrote a number of popular hymns. His translation of the Bible became the foundation of modern German.

Aftermath

In 1530, Charles V tried to restore order by calling another diet at Augsburg. By this time, Reformed, Mennonite, Anabaptist and other denominations were springing up all over Europe. Each group was asked to write down its teachings in a statement or confession.

On June 25, the Lutheran group presented a series of 28 articles. At the time, they did not realize that their statement, the Augsburg Confession, would become a basic creed for Lutherans.

The emperor rejected their position. He ordered church property returned to Roman bishops and forbade the Lutherans to continue with their work.

In 1531, the Lutherans joined with other Protestants to form the League of Schmalkalden. If necessary, they were prepared to go to war with Rome's supporters to defend their faith. The Turks had invaded Austria, and the emperor managed to get both the Protestants and the Roman Catholics to fight the Turks instead of each other.

However, armed conflict and the eventual division of Germany into Lutheran and Roman Catholic areas began in the summer of 1546. Luther had died on February 18 of that year.

Those other Lutherans

Lutherans in Canada are not one big happy family. As I told you at the beginning of this chapter, there are Lutherans in Canada who do not belong to the ELCIC.

The majority of these belong to the Lutheran Church—Canada (LCC). There are also a few Lutherans in independent congregations or in congregations which are part of some very small Lutheran groups.

At times, it has looked as though we were close to a family reunion. But whenever that has happened, a stubbornness in us seems to find new ways to keep the split going.

The Lutheran Church—Canada (LCC)

The Lutheran Church—Canada was formed in 1989 and has its roots in the Missouri Synod in the United States. The Missouri Synod grew out of the Lutheran Confession movement in Germany in the 19th century. These people left Germany because they were convinced that they could not practise their newly discovered faith in the conditions in which they found themselves at home.

The churches at home were state churches. Since you have just read some of the history of the early formation of those churches, you can appreciate that there was little tolerance for dissent. These state churches taught that religion simply involved living the good life. On top of that, in the territories of Prussia, the king forced the churches of Lutheran and Calvinist traditions to form a new united church.

So in the 1840s, these Lutheran dissenters came to Perry County, Missouri, and founded what became known as the Lutheran Church—Missouri Synod. Over the years, the Missouri Synod has been known for outstanding scholarship and a strong evangelism program.

A number of congregations in Canada, primarily German, were attracted to this synod because they wanted to have well-trained pastors. They were frustrated by the poor quality of pastors who sometimes plagued Canadian Lutheran congregations in the 19th century. There were no Canadian seminaries training Canadian pastors then. Some of the people who called themselves pastors were little better than saddlebums.

Sometimes, congregations fought about which

synod to join. These fights occasionally became so bitter that people were killed. The wounds left by these old battles still divide Lutherans in some communities.

However, this was not always the case. A number of Manitoba and Saskatchewan congregations found it hard to get a pastor. They were willing to take whoever would come and didn't quibble about the person's Lutheran label. These congregations simply joined whatever group the pastor happened to be from. The next time they needed a pastor, if the pastor was from a different group, they switched again.

Over time, Lutheran groups merged and remerged until it looked as if Lutherans would become one denomination in Canada. However, except for some smaller mergers into the Missouri Synod, the Canadian congregations in the Missouri Synod had never taken part in these mergers and continued to remain separate.

An attempt in Canada in the late 1960s and early 1970s appeared promising. Then both of the groups that eventually formed the ELCIC decided to ordain women. This was unacceptable to those who belonged to the Missouri Synod. Merger talks collapsed.

The leadership of the LCC has been trying to work with the leadership of the ELCIC to spell out our differences clearly. They want to get beyond painting caricatures and telling horror stories about each other. Some of the differences are very subtle. Others are more obvious.

Unlike the ELCIC, the LCC does not ordain women. In some LCC congregations, women are not allowed to vote or to hold office. The LCC also practises close or closed Communion.

While the ELCIC and most other Lutheran churches in the world belong to the Lutheran World Federation, the LCC does not. The LCC and a few sister Lutheran churches believe that the ELCIC's way of thinking is not completely true to Lutheran doctrine. They insist that there must be complete agreement in the gospel and all its ramifications before altar and pulpit fellowship is possible with another church.

This means that, although I am an ordained Lutheran pastor, I would not be invited to preach in an LCC congregation or to lead worship there. If I were to come forward to the altar to receive Holy Communion in an LCC congregation, I might be refused. The congregation might consider it inappropriate for me to receive Communion because I am not in church fellowship with that church.

A few LCC pastors have interpreted the idea of altar and pulpit fellowship very rigidly. They consider public prayer a form of worshiping together. So, if a meeting includes public prayer, they will not even attend that meeting if it includes non-LCC Lutherans, or any other Christians for that matter.

Inter-Lutheran cooperation

However, with the exception of a few rigid pastors and parishioners, Lutherans in Canada get along far better than what I've just said might lead you to expect.

The national headquarters of the ELCIC and of the LCC are located just a few blocks from each other in Winnipeg. Our leaders cooperate with each other and help each other out whenever they can.

We even have a structure to help us work together called The *Lutheran Council in Canada*. We are also very proud of the work that we share through *Canadian Lutheran World Relief*.

I rejoice at the positive contributions made by the Lutheran Church—Canada. I look forward to that day when there will be neither ELCIC nor LCC, a day when all of us will simply worship, witness, and celebrate together in God's family of faithful believers.

Chapter 11

Photo: Darrell Dyck

How the ELCIC works

If you want more than a nodding acquaintance with us, you have to know how we organize ourselves and how we make decisions. A lawyer once carefully studied the way the ELCIC operates. Afterward, he told me that we work so hard to do things democratically that he wonders how we ever get anything done.

We try to make sure that everyone in the ELCIC has a chance to take part in important decisions. There are many different structures and people in the ELCIC. So it can take a very long time before we reach a decision.

Living by grace is very important to us. That's why we believe in giving people as much freedom as possible. Whenever we can, even after the majority has reached a decision, we still allow people in our church to hold a different opinion or to do things in a different way. We would rather have dissenters come around to our way of thinking and acting in their own time than force them into something that they don't feel right about.

Membership

Every time we see the latest census figures, we get a surprise. We discover people who still count themselves as Lutherans even though congregations stopped counting them because they no longer participate.

Baptism automatically makes a person a member of the Lutheran congregation in which they were baptized. This includes all the rights and responsibilities that go with membership.

I need to make a distinction between membership and voting membership. Baptism makes a person a member and that holds true for all spiritual matters. However, when it comes to legal matters, congregations use a variety of ways to develop a list of voting members.

I've sat in a number of council meetings where a great deal of sweat and agony went into deciding to move someone from the active roll to the inactive roll. Later on, we spent just as much sweat and agony deciding whether to move the person from the inactive roll to the responsibility list. We really hate to be judgmental in any way.

Most congregations make it very easy to remain on the active roll. A person simply has to receive Communion once, or make a financial contribution of any sort, during the year. Twenty-five cents or one trip to Communion does the trick. A few eyebrows may raise, but the person stays on the roll.

Baptism is the key

Why is knowing who is a member so important to us? Membership is where we place the power. Each baptized member is a key part of the whole ELCIC.

Unfortunately, many of our members don't realize that. They don't know that we take their opinions seriously. Their role is important in making decisions. Yet

169

too many leave it to too few to take an interest in what happens.

Of course the ELCIC has a bureaucracy. Every organization this size needs one. The ELCIC faces the same realities and tensions as any other national organization in Canada. However, our small size means that our leaders are more accessible than might be possible in larger denominations. Church leaders are able to pay more attention to what people in the congregations are thinking.

Suppose a congregational member writes in and raises an important matter. Everyone who should know the writer's opinions usually reads that letter. Sometimes a good point raised by one or two letters results in a significant change.

Baptized members also have many other opportunities to share their views through the various structures of the church. To do so, they need to know how those structures work. Then they can help to get things done and to have their opinions count.

Baptized members are organized into congregations. The elected head of the congregation is a president or chairperson who also presides at congregational council.

ELCIC congregations use a variety of organizational patterns. They develop their structures to fit their local needs. Whatever the structure, it works best when everyone gets involved.

Synods and Conferences

The congregations belong to a synod. There are five of these in the ELCIC. The Eastern Synod includes congregations in Nova Scotia, New Brunswick, Quebec, and most of Ontario. The territory of the other synods is obvious from their names: The Manitoba-Northwestern Ontario Synod, The Saskatchewan Synod (although it includes a few Manitoba congregations), The Synod of Alberta and the Territories (includes Yukon and Northwest Territories), and The British Columbia Synod. A bishop is the elected head of each synod.

The congregations in a synod also are grouped

together into small geographic areas called conferences. The elected head of the conference is a dean who must be a member of the clergy.

Councils

At every level in the ELCIC, there is an elected governing body called a council. The congregation has a congregational council; the conference, a conference council; the synod, a synodical council; and the ELCIC, the church council. Most people in the ELCIC call their congregational council the church council. This doesn't really matter or confuse things unless you are trying to talk about actions taken by councils at the congregational and national levels.

These councils handle the routine decisions of the level of the church for which they are responsible. However, they act only through the authority that has been given to them by the people who elected them.

The whole group makes major decisions at a regularly held or specially convened meeting. At the congregational level, these are called congregational meetings and annual meetings. At the synodical and national level, they are called conventions.

A bishop told me that, after a convention reaches a decision, he feels duty bound to uphold and defend that decision. He keeps his personal opinions private, no matter how strongly he may personally disagree with that decision.

Some are more equal than others

I told you that we try to be very democratic. So you might be surprised to learn that, as a member of the clergy, I have more voting power than a layperson at every level of the ELCIC, except the congregational level. This is simply because our clergy have more chances to vote than our laypeople do.

In the congregation, a member of the clergy has one vote just like any other baptized member. However, it is not practical for every baptized member to attend and to vote at conference, synodical, and national meetings.

There would be too many people to get anything done. It would be too expensive. Besides, most people wouldn't show up to vote anyway.

We set the clergy aside for ministry and give them special training. We make it their business to take time to study and consider important theological matters. We give them the responsibility of guiding our decisions. With this in mind, we automatically make clergy official delegates to conference and synodical meetings. We expect them to attend those meetings unless they present a valid reason to be excused.

Lay delegates

We let the rest of the baptized off the hook. They select other laypeople as delegates to represent them at conference and synod meetings. We expect these lay delegates to study the issues just as hard as the clergy should. They try, as best they can, to represent the views of the people whom they represent.

The documents that a delegate may need to study are sometimes so thick that they are measured not by the number of pages, but by the inch. It amazes me to see how seriously most delegates take their responsibilities and how well informed most are about the issues that they vote on.

Some congregations hold special meetings with their delegates to talk things over and to give instructions before the delegates go to a meeting to vote. However, when the vote is taken, delegates must decide for themselves what they think is the right thing to do. This is because they may have learned more from the discussion at the meeting than might have been discussed back home.

National conventions

Every two years the ELCIC meets in convention. When the ELCIC formed, it decided that every parish should be represented at the national convention. Ideally this would mean that every member of the clergy as well as a suitable number of laypeople from every parish should be delegates.

Canada is very large and a number of our congregations are very small. The costs make such a convention
impracticable. So, in the Canadian way, a compromise
was worked out that, although it is a bit cumbersome,
seems to work.

Every parish (a parish is a congregation or group of
congregations served by one minister or ministerial
team) is entitled to one or more delegates. This depends
on the number of baptized people in that parish. Each
conference is asked to elect a certain number of clergy-
delegates. The number is calculated by looking at how
many baptized people there are. We make sure that
there will be more lay delegates voting than clergy
delegates. These clergy delegates then automatically
represent the parishes to which they belong.

After the clergy delegates are elected, each parish
whose pastor was not elected selects a lay delegate.
Some larger parishes are entitled to more than one
delegate. Some clergy are so popular that they would be
elected as clergy-delegates to every convention. So we
insist that the congregation must have a lay delegate at
least once every three conventions. This gives the
laypeople from that congregation a chance to get in on
the action.

If you followed that, great. You're in charge of
counting the ballots at the next conference meeting. I
haven't bogged you down with a lot of technical details
here because I hope you will finish this book. Often,
even those close to the action have to haul out the
constitution to sort out just what needs to be done.

The way we look in the media

Canadian media do not pay very much attention to
the ELCIC. Maybe it's because our name is too long to
print in the papers. The names of the people we elect are
sometimes hard to pronounce. It also has something to
do with our small size. Our decisions are important to us,
but not very important to most other people.

Reporting on religion is often a job assigned to an

inexperienced reporter. Often such rookies don't know anything about religion and are hoping to pull a new assignment quickly. There are a few papers in Canada who have good reporters on this beat. Those of us for whom church is important are grateful for their efforts.

My predecessor at Canada *Lutheran*, Ferdy Baglo, once noted that more people take part in church activities every week than those who take part in sporting events. But who gets all the press coverage?

The ELCIC doesn't make the news very often. Sometimes we do when we have done something with other Christian groups in Canada. Or when there is a scandal. Or when something controversial happens. Unfortunately, some of the people who put those stories together are more interested in getting a good story than in getting their facts straight. If you were as busy as they are and had as many stories to cover as they do, what you reported likely wouldn't be much different.

As editor of *Canada Lutheran*, it is my job to fill in some of the gaps that the other media don't have time to cover. I try to share the news and views that are of special interest and concern to people in the ELCIC.

No other national publication would tell you about the pros and cons involved regarding the ordination of diaconal ministers. But that is something our members want to know. Nor would the secular press likely share stories about how Christians' faith helps them or influences their decisions. We try to provide a Christian perspective on current issues such as free trade, immigration, and the like. We also share news about what the churches in Canada and around the world are doing.

The ELCIC also puts out a number of newsletters, pamphlets, and other documents to help interested people keep up with what is going on. These always come to at least the pastor. Congregational members tell us that some pastors never pass this material on. So you may have to take some initiative to keep informed about things that matter to you. Fortunately, when pastors know that someone is interested in a particular subject, most will share anything that comes their way.

174

Divisions and Offices

Now it's time for me to lead you through the alphabet soup. It seems that bureaucracies cannot survive without acronyms. The ELCIC is no exception.

Acronyms save trees. How many extra trees would have been paper if, instead of using the acronym ELCIC, I had written "the Evangelical Lutheran Church in Canada" throughout this book?

The first time you attend a committee meeting at any level of the ELCIC is an adventure. It feels as if you've stumbled upon a tribe of people who don't use English to communicate. "Has WLS had time to consider the implications of SACPRAC after DTEL got finished with it? Should we send copies to CCC, LWF and WCC for their information?"

There is no way to keep this from happening. Bureaucracies breed acronyms. The trick is to learn the code when you have to use it a lot.

When you don't know the code, learn to speak up. Ask, "Just what exactly is it that you are talking about?" It always turns out that most of the other people in the room were wondering exactly the same thing, but were too timid to ask.

To get all the work done the ELCIC has organized several divisions and offices. Depending on the size and sophistication of the synods, conferences and congregations, you will find these duplicated in some way on those levels as well. As I wrote this book, the ELCIC was beginning to rethink its structure. However, even if we change the structure or the acronyms, we will still have to do the things described here.

The Division for Canadian Mission (DCM) tries to sort out how Canada is growing. Then it launches new ministries in some of the places where new growth is taking place. In some cases this means gathering a group of people in a new suburb and organizing them into a congregation. At other times it means trying to get an established congregation to realize how the population in its neighborhood is changing. DCM may help them begin a ministry to the new people moving in. As jobs and communities spring up to develop Canada's resources in frontier situations, the ELCIC often works with the Anglican Church, the United Church, and the Presbyterian Church to establish shared ministries.

The Division for Church and Society (DCS) tries to keep the ELCIC and its leaders alerted to the changing social conditions around us. Sometimes it helps the church develop policies to guide people in dealing with these things. Often, the ELCIC does this in cooperation with other Canadian churches through interchurch coalitions.

The Division for College and University Services (DCUS) looks after campus ministry and the various schools related to the ELCIC: Augustana University College in Camrose, Alberta; Luther College at the University of Regina, as well as Luther College High School; and Lutheran Collegiate Bible Institute at Outlook, Saskatchewan, are institutions of the ELCIC.

The Division for Parish Life (DPL) is responsible for much of the work that most directly touches congregations. It develops such things as worship materials, witness programs, and educational program resources. It also looks after youth ministry and church camping. *Eternity for Today*, a quarterly devotional booklet, and *RACKET*, a newsletter for youth, are published by DPL.

The Division for Theological Education and Leadership (DTEL) develops the standards for ministry in the ELCIC. It works with the ELCIC's seminaries in providing theological education. The ELCIC has two seminaries: Lutheran Theological Seminary in Saskatoon, Saskatchewan; and Waterloo Lutheran Seminary in Waterloo, Ontario.

The Division for World Mission (DWM) provides missionary personnel in several places around the world. One of its programs (administered in partnership with DPL), Volunteers in Mission, is shared with the Anglican Church of Canada.

The name of **the Department of Finance and Administration** (DFA) describes its task. It makes sure that accurate records are kept for every penny people donate and sees that proper accounting procedures are followed.

The Office for Communication (OC) oversees the publication of *Canada Lutheran* and helps other offices and divisions to print most of their materials. Video productions made through the OC are another way that the ELCIC tells its story. Many of these are produced in large enough quantities to permit every ELCIC congregation to have one for its video library. Some are also shown on VISION TV and other cable channels.

The Office for Resource Development (ORD) looks after fundraising and friend-raising. ORD tries to educate all of us to be better stewards. It also administers the Global Hunger and Development Appeal (GHDA) which works in close cooperation with Canadian Lutheran World Relief.

The Committee for Pensions administers the ELCIC's pension plan for its clergy and layworkers.

The bishop and **the secretary** of the ELCIC work together very closely. The bishop's office oversees general administration of the church. The bishop is also responsible for ecumenical relationships with such groups as the Lutheran Council in Canada, the Lutheran World Federation, the Canadian Council of Churches and the World Council of Churches. The secretary's office shares in the overseeing of general administration as well as looking after legal and archival matters.

The bishop and the secretary, together with the vice-chairperson and the treasurer, are the officers of the church. The officers are responsible for making day-to-day decisions between church council meetings.

National and International partnerships

While many of us aren't very aware of church links beyond the ELCIC, these bonds do have an influence on our lives.

The ELCIC and the Lutheran Church—Canada (LCC) form the Lutheran Council in Canada. I talked about the LCC in the chapter "All in the family." This council makes it possible for us to work at some things together, such as chaplaincies and scouting. It also allows us to keep lines of communication open between our two denominations.

The ELCIC is one of about 114 member churches of the Lutheran World Federation (LWF) which has its headquarters in Geneva. Each member church is autonomous. Membership helps us to strengthen and clarify our Lutheran identity as well as to cooperate on some international projects.

Membership in the Canadian Council of Churches (CCC) helps the ELCIC to work with other Canadian denominations on important national issues. Two Lutherans, Norman Berner and Donald Sjoberg, have served as presidents of the CCC.

The ELCIC is also a member of the World Council of Churches (WCC). The work of the WCC has encouraged Lutherans in Canada to think about such things as sacramental and ministry practices, women's issues, aboriginal rights, economic justice, and care for the environment.

Cooperation

We are not a very big denomination. We don't have the resources to do all the things we would like to do. Some feel that this presents us with a unique opportunity because it forces us to cooperate with other Christians in Canada whenever we can.

That's why we work on social issues through the various Canadian church coalitions. We would never be able to do the necessary research without this arrangement.

At the time of writing this book, a number of our congregations were trying out a new lectionary intended for common use by Christian churches. We Lutherans had been using our own lectionary. This meant that we could not take part in developing some of the worship and teaching resources that other Canadian churches were sharing.

A denomination

You could probably spend your entire life as a member of a congregation in the ELCIC and not be very aware of any of the things I've been talking about in this chapter. You may even wonder, "What does this have to do with my relationship with God? Do we really need all this stuff?"

I think we do. That opinion has nothing to do with the fact that I collect a salary by being part of the bureaucracy.

Our relationship with God needs nourishment and strength. We receive this through the contacts we have with God's people. Congregations help our faith to grow by giving us other people of faith who share in our individual journeys. Just as we need other people to help us along the way, a congregation needs help to fulfill its mission in life.

Even congregations that call themselves "independent" need ways of doing denominational things. They need trained leaders, worship materials, teaching tools, and so on. Often they make use of what denominations have produced. They usually find it necessary to form alliances and to work together with others in formal or informal arrangements.

Still, it helps to take a long hard look at the way we do things every now and then. Committees spring up that keep on working long after their purpose for being has disappeared. Church bureaucrats learn to defend their budgets and their turf the same way that any other bureaucrats do. They sometimes forget the bigger picture.

One person who has been working in various denominational headquarters for a long time cautioned me against getting too excited about any talk of restructuring. He says that restructuring is a regular part of denominational life and that it happens almost predictably. He also claims that when the dust finally settles, you discover that a lot of time and energy has been spent getting back to doing what you were doing in the first place because these things have to get done.

Who is in charge here?

This is a good time for me to talk about something that people seldom talk about in church—power. Like it or not, whenever a group of people gets together to do anything, even to be a congregation, we have to talk about how power gets used or abused.

Serious problems sometimes happen in church structures over rather silly and insignificant issues. These problems use up a lot of energy and emotion because the issue being talked about is not the real issue. The real issue is often who is in charge around here? Who runs this show?

And when you think that you have God on your side, the whole thing really gets out of hand.

In the chapter "What we believe," I explained the Lutheran idea that we are simultaneously saint and sinner. Because we are simultaneously saint and sinner, power can be a problem.

In the ELCIC, as in any other organization, there are a few people who want to run things. These few are more interested in looking impressive than in doing anything particularly impressive. Fortunately there aren't many of these people around. In a small organization like the ELCIC, they are usually identified very quickly and seldom given any real power.

On the other hand, there are a number of people in our church who are born to be leaders. Paul has some good things to say about this in chapter 12 of his first letter to the Corinthians. You may want to read it over and think about it.

180

Dedicated leaders are a gift from God. They have a real ability to get things done and to help people work together. Most leaders in the ELCIC genuinely want to help make ministry happen.

If the lines of communication are kept open, if people trust each other, if everyone has a fair chance to take part in the decisions that they care about, and if no one is shut out from sharing in the leadership, then we don't get into problems with power. But those are many "ifs." They sometimes get neglected. That's why, even if all those meetings and committees and councils seem a bit tedious, they're still important.

When it comes to sharing power in the ELCIC, any baptized member is eligible for election. There are two exceptions: the role of bishop and dean which must be filled by an ordained person. Any ordained Lutheran can become a bishop or a dean. However, women, young people, new immigrants, and people who do not have college degrees are not represented in most of the ELCIC's decision-making bodies in proportion to their numbers.

As fair as I try to be, I really don't know what it means to be a black teenager, or a middle-aged Chinese woman recently arrived in Canada, or an elderly Estonian who came to Canada after the Second World War, or a newly ordained female pastor in this church. I doubt very much that any sort of quota system would make representation any fairer. The ELCIC continues to work at finding ways to share the power more fairly.

Sharing the decision-making

Whenever the ELCIC makes a significant decision about policy, it tries to ensure that everyone has had a chance to talk the matter over beforehand. This process can sometimes take several years. Even then, the outcome will not necessarily be as clear as one would expect.

For example, the ELCIC decided that there should be a "Statement on Sacramental Practices." A special committee was formed to study the matter and to prepare some recommendations. The ideas were shared with a number of people. Those people helped the committee to refine what needed to be said into a draft document. Study materials were sent out to every congregation with the request that people look things over carefully and get back to the committee with their comments. Many people did. Many meetings were held at all levels of the church to discuss the matter.

After several revisions and refinements, a recommendation was brought before the National Convention in Saskatoon in 1989. The delegates decided that people needed more time to think the matter over. The ELCIC spent two more years studying the material. Then, at the National Convention in Edmonton in 1991, after a lengthy and sometimes heated debate, the delegates finally approved the "Statement on Sacramental Practices."

Even so, after all this, the delegates to the Edmonton Convention passed a resolution that "the 'Statement on Sacramental Practices' as adopted is to be viewed as a guideline for congregations and is not binding on them."

Living with our differences

We Lutherans are a very mixed group of people. Our attitudes and opinions have been shaped by the regions we live in, who our ancestors were, and the kind of Lutheranism that we were brought up with.

There are many things in this book that I have said about Lutherans that other Lutherans would dispute. Some will likely be offended by the way I said it because it wasn't dignified enough. Or I didn't quote the Bible often enough. Some will cheer one section and jeer another.

Because of our differences, we don't resolve things as clearly as some would like. When something is ambiguous and can be seen from several different points of view that all seem to have some merit to them, we say so.

That doesn't always sit well with those who think that their point of view is clearly right and who want us to lay down the law and agree with them. Such talk usually makes me suspicious, especially when I'm the one using it. If a decision has to be forced onto people, is that really the right decision?

In the past, some who have had serious disagreements have walked away and formed their own groups. Such action is a terrible witness to the power of the gospel. Instead of being able to say, "Look at how much these Christians love each other," outsiders are simply left saying, "Look at these Christians!"

If we are really a church that believes in grace, then we have to learn to deal with each other as graciously as God deals with us. That's not always easy, but I think most of us in the ELCIC are making a real effort to do that.

When we disagree

Dissent is an honorable part of Lutheran tradition. Churches are not infallible. They have been known to make poor decisions. But while honest and carefully thought out dissent is one thing, negative reactions based solely on deeply held prejudices or comfortable ways of thinking or acting are quite another.

I was present when decisions were made about the ELCIC's position on abortion and "the Statement on Sacramental Practices." In both cases there was strong and vigorous debate. In both cases this point had been reached after several years of opportunity to study and debate the matters at every level of the ELCIC.

When the votes were taken, I was standing where I could see the entire floor. I saw overwhelming majorities carry both decisions. Yet there are those who claim that the votes were very close, that the decisions were rushed, and that people weren't given an opportunity to discuss these things. More to the point, I have heard some people complain about the decisions while admitting that they ignored the opportunity to speak up when they had the chance.

On the other hand, there were those who simply asked that their opposition be recorded so that everyone knew where they stood. Then they continued on in the church from there. Others found that the principle in question was just too important for them, and they left the ELCIC.

If people find the ELCIC's position uncomfortable and there is a denomination that matches their differing viewpoint, then that's the denomination to which they should belong. The ELCIC is unlikely to change its mind once it has made a decision as the result of a lengthy process such as the one I have described.

A word of caution, though. A pastor tells of serving two different Lutheran congregations in the same community. He was curious about why there were two and not one. He couldn't see any real difference between the two, and he was pastor of both.

When he asked one member for an explanation, the man replied that many years ago there had been only one congregation. Then a dispute developed. People quickly lined up on one side or the other. Feelings became so strong that the congregation finally divided over the matter. "So, which side of the issue does this congregation stand for?" asked the pastor.

The man paused, grew a bit red in the face, and mumbled, "I don't remember. I don't think anyone does."

My church home

I've tried to give you an honest picture of how the ELCIC works. I hope I have helped you to see that we are not perfect people. However, we are people who take God's grace very seriously, even in the way we run our church.

I have been a Lutheran living in Canada all my life. The particular Lutheran denominational hook that I have hung my hat on has changed three times since I was born. Each time, I, along with the other Lutherans who have been part of the mergers, have had to rediscover what being Lutheran in a Canadian context means.

ELCIC Lutherans represent a very new denomination. We are still sorting out exactly what we want to be. This ELCIC of ours may not even exist a few years from now. We may have decided that it would be better to be part of a new denomination that includes the rest of the Lutherans in Canada. Or even other Canadian Christians. Who knows?

For now I am content to share my membership with some very wonderful and dedicated people who have been gathered by God to be the Evangelical Lutheran Church in Canada. What happens to us next really depends on what God chooses for us.

There is a drawing somewhere that shows a family standing in a very untidy room in their home. Mom is trying to blow a curl out of her eyes that has fallen across her face. Dad looks as if he has been cleaning out the garage. The kids' clothes have been through a few playgrounds and puddles. Over them hangs a sign that reads "God bless this mess!" The whole family is beaming with love and radiating joy at each other's company.

That's the way I feel about our ELCIC household of faith. This is where I feel at home. This is the place where I have been welcomed and raised, and where I know that I am loved.

Chapter 12

Photo: Kenn Ward

Learning to speak Lutheran

If you are a sports fan, you know that if you really
want to understand the game you have to learn the
language. Baseball has "balls" other than the little
round one they hit and throw. Football has "downs"
that are not the opposite of ups. Basketball has a
"court" that has nothing to do with lawyers.

I've never been able to understand what "love" has
to do with tennis, or what "birdies" and "eagles" have to
do with golf. Hockey, lacrosse, darts and all the others
have their own words. You have to understand the
words if you want to enjoy the game.

We Lutherans also have our own special set of words.
Many of them are used by other Christians as well. This
chapter is meant to help you learn our language.

Don't worry if you can't remember all of them. There won't be a test at the end. Many Lutherans don't know or don't use all of them either. But speaking at least a bit of the lingo will help you to feel more at home.

When in doubt, nod your head knowingly and follow the crowd. If you are really brave, you can always ask someone, "What does that word mean?" Maybe you'll both learn something from the answer.

I've tossed in some hints about how to pronounce some of the ones that I thought might give you trouble. I'm not an authority on pronunciation so you might want to check it out with someone in your local Lutheran congregation. Then again, maybe they won't be exactly sure either. That's one of the beauties of being Lutheran. There's always something new to learn.

Absolution (AB-so-loo-shun)—The part of confession and forgiveness where the pastor tells you that you are forgiven.

When you hear that absolution, you can bet your life on it. Jesus did.

Acolyte (AK-oh-light)—The people, usually in their early teens, who light the candles and help out in the worship service in a variety of ways. It comes from a Greek word meaning "one who follows."

You can tell the difference between these people and the ushers. Besides rushing up at the last minute and lighting the candles when the acolyte didn't show up, the ushers don't wear gowns. It is fun to watch an awkward youngster develop poise and confidence over a year or two of helping out this way.

Advent (ADD-vent)—Means "a coming or an arrival." A short season in the Church Year, lasting the four Sundays before Christmas, when we remember that Christ is coming again.

Alb—The white gown that the pastor wears. In some congregations, you will also see other worship leaders wearing albs. The word comes from the Latin "white."

This gown has only been in use in Lutheran churches for a few years so you may see other garb worn by the pastor, especially if he is an older pastor, or you are worshiping in a Lutheran church that still holds onto ties with a European tradition. (I'm not being sexist here. The ordination of women and the use of the alb came in at about the same time. As far as I know all our women clergy wear albs.)

Altar—A name that is often used for the communion table. Because Holy Communion is celebrated at the altar, it is sometimes called "the Sacrament of the Altar."

Amen—"So be it!" Saying "amen" is like signing your name on the line at the bottom of an important agreement.

However, there is some disagreement whether to say AY-men or AH-men, but I'm not aware of any Lutheran group splitting to form a new denomination over this debate...yet.

Antiphonal (an-TIFF-phone-al)—This involves singing psalms or canticles in two parts, with one group singing in response to the other. Sometimes the choir sings, and then the congregation sings, and then back to the choir and so on. The word comes from a Greek word meaning "voice after voice." Sometimes readings are also done this way.

Apology of the Augsburg Confession—You may want to skip this until you find out what the Augsburg Confession is.

Apology comes from the Greek word *apologia* which means words, or a speech in defense.

After the Augsburg Confession was printed, the critics pointed out what they saw as flaws in it. (After all, isn't that what critics are supposed to do?)

The Apology tried to set the record straight by answering the critics. It was written by Philip Melanchthon and was published in 1531. (Melanchthon was a lot more diplomatic than Luther, so maybe apology is a good word. I can't imagine Luther apologizing for anything.)

Assisting minister—This role is becoming increasingly common in Lutheran services. It is the title for the layperson who helps to lead worship. However, preaching and presiding at the Sacraments are reserved for the pastor.

Augsburg Confession—Sounds like Lutherans are an exciting bunch of people, doesn't it? Sorry. You won't find this on the magazine rack next to *The National Enquirer*.

This statement, dated 1530 A.D., tried to explain that those who followed Luther were not teaching or doing anything that went against what was in the Bible, and that what they taught and did was in the best tradition of the catholic church. (See also "confession.")

Banns—This word from the Anglo-Saxon "to proclaim" describes the announcement that the pastor makes telling everyone that two people intend to get married and inviting the congregation to pray for the couple.

The announcement sometimes also contains that "If anyone can show just cause why these two should not be married..." Everyone holds their breath and crosses their fingers.

Baptism—The sacrament of initiation into the Church that uses water.

When our son Jef was very young, he thought that we were "bathsizing" the baby.

Baptistry—This isn't a tree planted by a Baptist or what Baptists call their clergy. It's the place where there is a baptismal font. (See Font, page 195.)

Benediction (ben-a-DIC-shun)—This is the blessing that the pastor gives at the end of the service. It is sometimes followed by "Go in peace. Serve the Lord."

189

I was always a bit suspicious when the congregation got really enthusiastic about replying "Thanks be to God." Were they cheering for the chance to serve, or to go?

Benevolence (ben-EV-oh-lents)—A word which sometimes appears on offering envelopes and/or in a congregation's financial reports. Money contributed to benevolence is sent to the synod, which then sends a portion of the contribution on to the national church, so that the synod and the national church can do their jobs.

Bishop—What we call the senior elected official of the synods and of the ELCIC. It is not true that the standard operating principle of our church reads: "If there is a problem, blame the bishop." It just seems that way to them.

Call—The official invitation by a congregation or an organization for a minister to serve as bishop, pastor, or diaconal minister. It is also used to describe the special sense of calling that people have about their vocation.

Calling—This is the reason God put you here, the role that you are meant to play in life.

Being a plumber, a pianist, a pizza maker, or a pastor are all callings. So is being a good parent, citizen, community leader, or friend.

Canticle—You will find some of these at the start of the hymn section of the *Lutheran Book of Worship.* They are songs, other than the Psalms, that usually come from the Bible.

Some of them are a bit tricky to learn, but with practice they can add a new musical sound to worship. Without practice, they sound like something else.

Cantor—A song leader.

Not to be confused with that person in the congregation who loudly belts out the hymn—off key.

Catechism (KAT-i-kism)—A summary of the important teachings in our religion that is set out in question and answer form. Luther wrote both a Small and a Large Catechism. Both are worth reading and learning.

Catechumen (kat-i-CUE-men)—Someone who is learning his or her catechism because that person is planning to join the church.

Catholic—It describes the universal, Christian Church. When it is used with a capital "C," it usually refers to the Roman Catholic Church.

We are trying to recover the word "catholic's" historic use and meaning. Unfortunately, some Lutherans have trouble with this word because of a deeply rooted prejudice against Roman Catholics.

I once had a mother show up at a congregation I was serving. She had driven many miles to ask me to teach her sons the catechism because there was no Lutheran church in her area. When I asked why she didn't pick a closer church for Christian instruction, say an Anglican one, she answered, "Because they use the word "catholic" when they say the Creed. "I guess you haven't been in a Lutheran church for a long time," I said, and opened the worship book to the Apostles' Creed. She took one look at the word "catholic" printed there, stormed out the door, and I never saw her again.

Censer (SEN-sir)—This has nothing to do with someone deciding what we should or should not be able to read or see in church. A censer is a closed container in which incense is burned. It hangs on the end of a chain or chains and is waved about to waft the smell of incense around.

However, many Lutheran congregations censor the use of a censer.

Chalice (CHAL-iss)—The cup used in Holy Communion for the wine. Surprise! It comes from a Latin word meaning "cup."

By the way, here's a piece of trivia that you can use to stump even the pastor. On many chalices there is a knob on the stem to make it easier to handle. It is called a "knop."

Chancel (CHANCE-el)—the altar area of a church.

Chant—This comes from Latin meaning "to sing." It is a liturgical song, sometimes a greeting or a prayer, usually sung without a musical instrument.

Some people have a chant so heavenly and swell; but others sound like the place where saints are loath to dwell.

Chasuble (CHAWS-you-bl)—This is a poncho-like piece of clothing that the presiding minister sometimes wears over an alb at Holy Communion. They can be very plain or incredibly ornate.

Chrismon—A white Christmas tree ornament made in the shape of a Christian symbol, often decorated with gold and silver glitter and jewelry.

Our daughter Teri-Lyn has a special Christmas tree decorated with the chrismons she has been receiving from her godmother each Christmas. Her godmother has been making one for her each year since Teri-Lyn was born.

Christening—A non-Lutheran term sometimes mistakenly used to talk about Baptism. This refers to the naming of a child or a ship. While this was once a common practice at the time of Baptism, it is now more a formality than a necessity.

Church—When Lutherans use Church with a capital "C," they mean the entire Christian Church, all baptized Christians. When they use it with a small "c," they mean a denomination, a congregation, or the building where the congregation worships.

Cincture (SINK-ture)—The rope belt used with an alb. My cincture has been known to lasso chairs and altar rails landing me flat on my back or causing me to drag a chair along behind me.

Cluster—A sub-grouping of congregations within a conference.

Communion—This Sacrament is so rich in meaning that I hesitate to try to give it a definition. By eating the bread, drinking the wine, and hearing the Word, Christians are nourished in the promise of salvation. Other names you may hear are the Eucharist, the Lord's Supper, the Sacrament of the Altar, the Mass, the holy meal. Some also talk about coming to the Lord's Table.

I prefer to talk about "receiving" Communion rather than "taking" Communion because this emphasizes what God does for us rather than what we do. (Incidentally, we use a capital "C" when using Communion as a noun and a small "c" when it's an adjective.)

Conference—This is not something you do on the telephone with a group of people, but a geographic grouping of congregations within a synod.

Confession—Surprisingly, Lutherans use this word two different ways. Confession, private or public, can be used to admit to the wrong things of which you are guilty, after which you receive absolution.

However, confession can also mean to witness. When Lutherans talk about the Confessions, we mean a statement or summary that bears witness to what the church believes and teaches. The Lutheran Confessions are found in *The Book of Concord*.

Confirmand (CON-fur-mand)—Since most Lutherans are baptized when they are babies, at some point in their lives, usually during their teens, they attend confirmation class so that they can learn about the basic teachings of the church. These classes are meant to prepare them for a service when they confirm or affirm the faith that was given to them as a gift at Baptism. The people who attend these classes are called "confirmands."

One pastor who was elected bishop is reported to have beamed and said, "Hallelujah! Does this mean I don't have to teach confirmation class any more?" Fortunately, that opinion is not universally shared by all pastors (although each one probably has such moments).

Congregation—A group of baptized Lutherans who are formally organized and officially recognized by the Lutheran church.

Credence (CREE-dense)—This is a table or shelf where the sacramental vessels are kept until they are carried to the altar for Holy Communion. You are more likely to hear people call it "the table for the communion ware."

Crucifer (CREW-sif-ur)—This person carries the processional cross if there is a procession during the worship service.

Diet of Worms—An important part of the Lutheran menu. Diet means "parliament" and Worms was the place where the parliament met for the famous heresy trial of Martin Luther.

Easter—A season in the Church Year of seven Sundays when the resurrection of Jesus Christ from the dead is specially celebrated (although every Sunday is considered "a little Easter").

The Sunday often called Easter Sunday is the first of these seven Sundays and is named "The Resurrection of our Lord."

Ecumenism (e-KYOUM-en-ism)—The promotion of Christian cooperation and unity. Ecumenical (EK-you-men-ikl) is the adjective.

194

Epiphany (ee-PIFF-an-ee)—Means "an appearance or a manifestation." A festival celebrated on January 6 when we remember the visit of the Magi to see the baby Jesus. Jim Taylor tells me that sometimes people say it when they mean "insight" or "realization."

The season in the Church Year that follows January 6 is also called Epiphany. Its length depends on the timing of Easter.

Eucharist (YOU-kar-ist)—This comes from a Greek word meaning "thanksgiving" and is a name sometimes used for the service of Holy Communion.

After a Lutheran Communion service which was attended by a number of people from other denominations, I overheard a Presbyterian minister say, "So that's why they call it **celebrating** the Eucharist!"

Evangelical—Evangelical is a word deeply rooted in our history. It means "those who share good (or God's) news." Notice the word "angel" in the middle? See "Gospel."

Flagon—The proper name for the pitcher used to hold the wine for Holy Communion.

In one of my congregations, the people who looked after the altar kept calling it "that thing that looks like a fancy coffee pot."

Font—The piece of furniture that holds the water for baptisms. Some hold a lot of water and some very little.

However they should never be used as a flower vase as I have seen done once or twice by people who didn't know what the font was for.

Gospel—While this word can be a shorthand way of talking about the good news of Jesus Christ, it is also used as a name for the first four books of the New Testament—Matthew, Mark, Luke, and John.

Lutherans stand to hear the Gospel being read at worship as a sign of the special respect that they hold for it. However, if it is a really long reading, as happens once or twice a year, we admit that the spirit is willing but the flesh is weak and sit for those readings of the Gospel.

Grace—If you don't learn any other word, learn this one. This is basic if you want to learn to speak Lutheran. It is even better when you experience it and learn to live it.

It means "love," but it's a whole lot richer and deeper than the things we often associate with love. However, if you take the best parts of what you know about love, you are getting very close to grace.

The best way that I know to learn about grace is to study what God did and does for us through Jesus.

Green Book, The—This has nothing to do with ecology. It's just a nickname that we give to the *Lutheran Book of Worship.*

Holy Communion—see Communion.

Holy Week—The week before Easter in the Church Year.

Host—Don't get excited if you hear someone talking about receiving the host. That means that the pastor is going to give you a communion wafer or a piece of communion bread. This is the "host."

Does this mean that people are forming a "receiving line" when they are standing around the altar for Communion?

Hymns—The songs we sing at worship.

Contrary to popular belief, pastors do not sit up nights searching through the hymn book to find hymns that no one has ever heard of and few people, other than trained musicians, can sing.

Incarnate (in-KAR-knit)—One of my favorite words. It means "in the flesh." Jesus was God in the flesh, a real flesh and blood human being.

Incense—An aromatic substance which gives a pleasant smell when burned.

Although the use of incense at worship has a long history, a number of the faithful get quite incensed at the suggestion that incense will be used at a service which they attend.

Installation—The ceremony where a person is officially "sworn in" and assumes office. Sometimes called "induction" or "covenanting" in other denominations.

Intern—A seminarian who is serving in a parish under a pastor's supervision so that he or she can gain some practical experience.

A girl was heard calling to the intern, "Hey you, almost a minister." She had things just about summed up.

Intinction (in-TINK-shun)—Some people prefer to dip the host into the communion wine rather than sipping from the common cup. This is called intinction. It is sometimes a very helpful way for sick people to commune.

Invocation (IN-voh-kay-shun)—The beginning part of a service when the pastor says, "In the name of the Father, and of the Son, and of the Holy Spirit." This is done to remind us in just whose name we are meeting.

This is not to be confused with the weather report that some pastors give at the start of a service. You know, when they say, "Good morning."

Lectern (lect-URN)—An extra reading desk that you may see in some congregations. Often it is used by lay people; the pulpit is then reserved for use by the pastor.

Lectionary (lec-SHUN-air-ee)—These are a pattern of Bible readings that have been selected for worship, public and private, during the year. The *Lutheran Book of Worship* follows a three-year cycle for Sunday services.

The book where these lessons have been printed to

make things easier for those who use them is also called a lectionary.

Lent—A season in the Church Year lasting the six weeks before Easter.

Liturgy (LIT-ur-jee)—a set form for worship that usually includes a number of historical texts and music that have been used in the Church for centuries. This word comes from a Greek word which means "work of the people."
 If you do liturgy, you're being "liturgical" (li-TUR-jikl).

Lord's Supper—Another name for the Sacrament of Holy Communion.

Luther, Martin—He's the person who got this whole Lutheran business started, although he hated the idea of a church being named after him and preferred the term "evangelical."

Lutheran Church—Canada—This is a different denomination than the ELCIC and has about 84,000 baptized members. We work together on a number of things such as **Canada Lutheran World Relief**, and military chaplaincy.

Manse—see "parsonage."

Mass—We haven't switched to physics class. Historically, this was the name for the communion service and is still used by Scandinavian Lutherans among others. The word probably comes from the Latin service where the priest said, "Missa est." (You are dismissed.)

Maundy Thursday—This is what we call Thursday in Holy Week. It comes from the Latin word for "commandment." At the service on Maundy Thursday, we remember Jesus' new commandment to "love one another as I have loved you."

Ministerial—An organization of ministers. Sometimes it is also called a **ministerium**.

Missal (MISS-l)—This is not some type of rocket. It is the big book with the worship services that the minister uses to lead worship. The print is in big letters so that the pastor can stand back, glance at the words and have his or her hands free.

The missal stand is the name of the book holder for the missal, but you probably guessed that.

Narthex—The entrance to the worship space where everyone stands around and visits if there is enough room. Really smart congregations have a narthex at least as big as their worship area.

Nave—This is the part of the church where the congregation sits. It is between the chancel and the narthex.

Offertory (OFF-ur-tory)—A song sung as the offering is being brought forward and the altar is being prepared for Holy Communion.

Ordination—A religious rite that makes a person a pastor. At the time of writing, the ELCIC was still deciding whether or not to have a separate ordination for bishops and whether or not to ordain diaconal ministers.

Pall (paul)—A large cloth usually decorated with a cross, and sometimes with other Christian symbols, which is used to cover the casket at a funeral service.

Paraments (PAIR-a-ments)—The cloths used on the altar, pulpit, and lectern.

Parish—A group of congregations served by the same pastor or pastors. Just to confuse things, sometimes we also use this word to talk about one congregation. It's important to know the difference because the term comes up when we decide how to elect delegates to our National Conventions.

Parishioner—A word sometimes used to describe a member of a congregation.

Parsonage—A name for the house where the pastor lives. Most Lutherans prefer this term as opposed to its alternative, **manse**. I'm not sure why, since we seldom refer to our clergy as parsons, although they are persons. Then again, since clergy can be male or female, we would hardly want to call it the "man's," would we?

Paschal candle (PASS-kl)—A large candle used during Easter to proclaim that Jesus is alive and among his people. It is also used at baptisms and funerals to remind us of our dying and rising with Christ. At other times, it stands, unlit, next to the baptismal font.

Pastor—This is what we call our clergy (at least within earshot). When talking to a member of the Lutheran clergy, it is always proper to call them "Pastor..." or "Mr., Ms., Miss, Mrs." (depending upon the sex and political orientation of the pastor).

"Reverend" is used only when writing to or about the pastor and never in talking to them. We also never call the pastor "the reverend." That's a sure sign that you haven't learned to speak Lutheran.

Pentecost—The birthday of the Church. Also the name of the last season in the Church Year when the Sundays are numbered as Sundays after Pentecost.

When you get somewhere around the Twenty-third Sunday after Pentecost, you often begin to wonder why the people who planned the Church Year couldn't have added an extra festival or two to liven things up. Fortunately, there are Thanksgiving and Reformation and a few other excuses that creative pastors come up with to perk things up.

Pericope (per-IC-oh-pea)—Parts of the Bible assigned for reading during the service.

Prelude (PRAY-lewd)—The stuff that comes right before the service when everyone is gawking around to see who is there or trying desperately to figure out what the pastor and the organist cooked up for this Sunday.

If you can get past all that, it can be a time to prepare for worship, a time for prayer and meditation, for looking over the planned order of the service so that you can fully take part in it and appreciate it, and for just being inspired by the music.

In practice, it usually turns out somewhere between both those ideas.

Procession—A sort of liturgical parade at the beginning of the service which usually involves the leaders of the service but, on such occasions as Palm Sunday, may include the entire congregation. Who says that dressing up in fancy costumes is only for children or Halloween?

Pulpit—The reading desk where the pastor often stands to preach the sermon or to read from the Bible. Many pulpits hold a copy of the Bible to show that what is said or read from that place is centered in the Word of God.

One enterprising congregation where I visited also had a clock hanging behind the pulpit. They had tried to hang it where the preacher could see it so he would shorten his sermons. When that didn't work, they hung it where they could see it.

Reformation—A big deal for Lutherans. Martin Luther tacked up 95 theses or ideas for reform in the church that he thought it would be a good idea to talk about. Things have never been the same since.

Strangely enough, Lutherans, for whom the Reformation is such a big deal, are sometimes very much against any suggestion of reform or change when their own church is mentioned. More than one pastor has been known to remark that the seven last words of a dying church are "We never did it that way before."

Reformed—This word hasn't been part of Lutheran vocabulary in Canada. It describes another tradition started by John Calvin, a contemporary of Martin Luther.

Calvin and Luther had some discussions to see if they could bring their two movements together but they couldn't reach an agreement. In a number of places around the world, however, Lutheran and Reformed churches have merged or are in the process of merging.

Responsibility list—When some congregations remove inactive members from their roll of members, they place them on a responsibility list. The congregation will no longer expect anything from that person. However, if the person should need the congregation, the congregation still feels a responsibility for that person and will try to help if called on.

Rite—These are important religious ceremonies such as marriage, ordination and confirmation, but do not have all the necessary ingredients to make them sacraments.

Sacrament—Commanded by Christ, these religious rituals give us the grace of God. These "means of grace" were given to assure us that the grace that Christ promised is as real as the water that washes us in the Sacrament of Baptism, or the bread and wine we eat in the Sacrament of Holy Communion. We have Jesus' word on it.

Salvation—The root meaning of this word is health or wholeness. When you are completely healthy and whole in body, mind, soul and spirit, and in your relationships with God and humanity, that's salvation. That's also something only Jesus can give us.

As I wrote down these definitions in my computer, every now and then I had to "save" the information so that it wouldn't get lost. Because of the salvation that is ours through Christ Jesus, we will never be erased from heaven's memory bank.

Sanctuary—This is the area right around the altar (inside the altar rail if there is one). You will hear many of us mistakenly use this word for the entire worship space (often including me).

Seminary—A school for pastors.

Some people confuse seminary with cemetery; they seem to think that both places hold a lot of stiffs.

Seminarian—A student who attends a seminary.

Sometimes they actually learn something while they are there, much to the relief and amazement of their teachers.

Sermon—A speech by the pastor during the service which is supposed to enlighten the listeners about God's will for their lives.

Some sermons have been known to inspire people to greatness; others have led people to such peace of mind that they have drifted off into a pleasant slumber and gently snored their way to the final blessed "amen."

Sex—Something Lutherans enjoy along with the rest of the population and which gives us as much joy and despair as anyone else. How much we talk about sex depends on whom we are talking to.

Sin—This is not all those little things we do wrong. Those are sin**s**. Sin is the evil reality in our lives that is part of us and results in our committing sins. The Apostle Paul helped me understand how real sin is and how it works with these words: "I can will what is right, but I cannot do it. For I do not do the good I want, but the evil I do not want is what I do." (Romans 7:18b,19)

Stewardship—What we do with what we've got. This includes how we make use of our time, spend our money, and exercise our abilities—all of which are gifts from God.

Synod (sin-id, not sinODD, as in "Forgive us, Lord, for we have synod.")—A major geographic grouping of congregations with a bishop at its head. There are five synods in the ELCIC.

Thurible—A container for burning incense, though why anyone would want to do so is strongly disputed in many Lutheran congregations. Unlike a censor this just sits there.

Tithing—Giving 10 percent of your money off the top to the work of God. It's not a rule, but it is a good target to aim for and beyond.

Triduum—You won't run into this in most congregations. It is a term that describes a three-part celebration during Holy Week that begins on Maundy Thursday, continues on Good Friday, and ends with Easter Vigil.

Trinity—Describes the basic Christian understanding of God as God the Father, God the Son, and God the Holy Spirit.

Some Christians are trying to find suitable substitutes for the male words "Father" and "Son" out of concern that this language sounds sexist. Others are concerned that tampering with the traditional words would be as irreverent as the hippie in the 60s who talked about the Trinity as "Daddyo, Junior, and Spook."

Vicar—A name Lutherans sometimes give to their interns.

(Don't you just hate it when a reference book makes you look up another word to find out the meaning of the word that you were looking up in the first place?)

Wittenberg—The place where Martin Luther taught at university.

Word and Sacrament—This phrase sums up a complete Lutheran worship service as well as the most important function of a Lutheran congregation, namely that the Word of God is preached and taught faithfully, and that the Sacraments are properly celebrated.

Lutherans care very deeply about these things because these are the ways that God has given us to help everyone know that they can really count on God's grace and mercy.

Unfortunately, Lutherans also have a tradition of being so concerned about the "faithfully" and "properly" bit that they sometimes split into separate groups, each claiming that they have the faithful and proper stuff figured out more purely than the others do.

Word, The—This is used to mean three different things: the entire Bible, or the basic biblical message, or Jesus himself.

Chapter 13

Kenn Ward

So what?

When I was first learning to preach, my professor, Ed Riegert, taught me that I should never quit working on my sermon until I had asked myself the question, "So what?" If my sermon answered that question, then I could be satisfied that I had finished the job.

I've told you a great deal about the ELCIC and about myself as a member of the ELCIC. Now comes the time to ask, "So what?"

Finishing the job

Do you remember way back near the beginning of this book that I said I hoped to get you thinking, talking, and acting? I hope that you did do some thinking and that along the way you talked with a few people about what you've been reading.

Now it's up to you and me to act on what I've been writing about. Every now and then I get really upset with all the rotten things that are going on in the world and I moan, "Why doesn't somebody do something?"

Then I realize that that somebody needs to be me. A wise man once told me that if, at the end of your life, you can look back and find that you have accomplished more than five percent of everything that you hoped to achieve, you can count yourself a very lucky person.

It is impossible for me to right all the wrongs in this world that need righting. But I do have a few God-given gifts that can make a difference if I pick my issues wisely and well.

Change me, Lord

I remember one evening when a bunch of kids in our neighborhood did something wrong and my dad came out of the house and gave everyone a big lecture about right and wrong and how important it was that we know the difference if we wanted to grow up to be decent people. I was pretty embarrassed at the time, and I squirmed as some of the kids snickered.

But he took a stand for what he believed, even if it was just in front of a group of snickering kids. How much of him rubbed off on me, I wonder?

Before we try to change the world, we need to be sure that we are on the right side. Sometimes the only thing we can change is our own attitude. But that change can have so many important consequences.

A little prayer that I learned a while ago has made a big difference for me: "Change me, Lord."

I discovered that in order to pray that prayer, you have to admit that you might need changing. It becomes a prayer of confession and discovery.

I also pray that prayer because I have confidence that God can get through to me. It's part of my confession of faith. I believe that God will help me to see in myself what God sees in me.

207

Not alone

For me the biggest bonus of being an active member of the ELCIC is the constant reminders I get that I am not alone. Just when I get really discouraged and think that maybe life is a crazy crap shoot after all and that we are all a bunch of losers who are kidding ourselves, someone in the church reminds me that love and hope are still alive, that God is still in charge.

Wilfrid Laurier said that the 20th century would belong to Canada. It didn't quite work out that way. We are nearing the end of one of the most violent, destructive centuries in the history of humankind. We face an uncertain future.

Now more than ever we need to know that we are not alone. We need to be reminded that love and hope are still alive, that God is still in charge...

My favorite way of parting is to say "See you later. God bless." I used to use that regularly when I made hospital visits. It always amazed me how often and how sincerely I heard "God bless you too, pastor" in return.

I meant those words. They are at the core of my personal beliefs. I do believe that we will meet face to face one day in the company of our loving God. And I do believe that God intends to bless you.

See you later. God bless.